PASSIONS TRILOGY

UNCOMMON DEVOTIONAL READINGS
FOR EACH OF THE SEASONS

ADVENT / LENT / UNLENT

J. R. LARSEN

To Ben and Candace
with gratitude for your
friendship !

Carolyn

Published by Park Avenue Press
Yakima, Washington, United States of America
www.parkavepress.com

Book Cover Design by Franziska Haase.

ISBN 978-0-9995526-0-5
   1. Spiritual formation. 2. Devotional reading.

Printed in the United States of America
FIRST EDITION

to Stone
and
to Amanda Fay

*two of the most innately spilling-over-with-
passion humans I know*

*Your rooted strength and robust tenderheartedness
entreat and inspire me to do again each day the
wondrous and wretched work that God
has uniquely imprinted upon me to do.*

Introduction

Devotional readings are a special and sacred literary genre. On the one hand, they are simple – they are small collections of the thoughts and ideas and inspirations of ordinary people in ordinary time. But on the other hand, they are vastly complex. They are complex because they are about God, a God that is still both known and unknown, a God that came-to-earth and is yet mysterious. All of humankind lingers on the eternal voyage to discover who this God will turn out to be.

All literature holds the potential to change you, but devotional readings aim directly at that very thing. And isn't it usually the ordinary things that most profoundly impact us? Extraordinary experiences come and go, but the most radical life changes we ever make are usually the everyday ones, the ones that are scarcely noticeable to anyone but us, the ones that are hard fought and barely won. And, since the strength of God is the only force strong enough to reform the human heart, devotional writings hold an incredible potential to assist God in doing what only God can do – transform us from the inside out.

But change is hard. To allow ourselves to be changed on the inside often comes at great personal cost. Our pride and our comforts, our sensibilities and our relationships are often maimed in the process. It is distressing, awkward, magnificent work. How else can it be? We all, in our own ways, resist it, avoid it, and despise it.

We resist it until we have our first teeny experience of the freedom of actually becoming a new person. It is this freedom that convinces us that all of the pain was, if not worth it, at least for Good. Then, gradually, we surrender ourselves to the One who is, has been, and always will be to us devoted-to-death. We find that we can trust God to do gently the work that must be done in our inner lives if we are ever going to grow up in Life and Love. We find warm and

8

grateful affections for God growing within us – we are becoming more *devoted* to God. And we find in our souls a more mindful, active commitment to God's ways – we are becoming more *devoted* to God.

After all, why else do we read devotionals?

And, now, if you're at all still interested, I offer you my devotional trilogy. I hope you really enjoy it. And, because I hope that God will use it to change you, I hope you kind of hate it.

Book 1

Passions of Christ's Advent

Introduction
Passions of Christ's Advent

Advent is the proper liturgical name for what most of us call Christmastime. Every year, the moveable Advent season begins on the Sunday nearest to November 30 (the feast of St. Andrew the Apostle) and spans four Sundays. Therefore, it begins no earlier than November 27 and no later than December 3. The following twelve devotionals are intended to be read during the Advent season.

Some readers will choose to begin to read early in December, reading one devotional every other day or so, finishing on Christmas Day. Others will want to wait to begin on December 14 and enjoy one reading every day for the true 12 days of Christmas.

Though these twelve passions are arranged chronologically, according to the narratives of Jesus' birth, they stand alone -- each in its own

right. Some readers will find it unconsciona-
ble to read them in any order other than their
chronological order; others might benefit to
read them with a bit more spontaneity, select-
ing whichever passion is most fitting or most
needful for the day at hand. All that to say: thou
art loosed to choose whichever reading style
will suit you best.

Each devotional reading takes a close look at
one predominant emotion in the life of a person or group of persons who were somehow in-
volved in the birth of Jesus. My hope is that,
through unfettered, unedited emotion, the story itself will seem more real, more human, and
more relevant for today's reader. Furthermore,
my prayer is that each of us would see ourselves
in the story, that we would feel both affirmed
and challenged by the passions we find here,
and, above all else, that we would be drawn to
love more devotedly that Babe in the manger.

As we stare into the emotional states, the body
language, and the heart attitudes of these one
dozen first century Jesus-followers, let us also
take a hard look into our own interior lives. Let
us not fail to ask ourselves: What is my pas-
sionate response to the terrific and terrifying
reality: "Emmanuel - God Himself - has come
to live with us"?

14

"And Mary said,
'Behold, I am the servant of the Lord;
let it be to me according to your word.'"

Luke 1:38

the *self-sacrifice* of Mary

This can't have been the way Mary dreamed of starting her family: as the mother of an, apparently, bastard child, and as a recipient of all of the judgment and marginalization that goes with it.

How about you? Where has your life turned out differently than you'd planned? Where is there disappointment and heartache, even as you follow God?

Over the years, I've had to wrestle deeply with the following:

• Am I open-handed with my plans for my life or am I holding on with white-knuckles to my way?

• When He asks me to follow Him, will I even be listening? And will I say "yes" to wherever He leads?

• Will I "own," love, enjoy, and be grateful for my life even with God orchestrating it? Even when it's hard?

Let us learn to pray Mary's prayer out of the places of heartache and disappointment we face today. Jesus, too, learned this prayer, probably from His sweet mama. When facing the heartache of Death itself, (Matthew 26:39) "…. Jesus fell on his face and prayed, saying, 'My Father, if it be possible, let this cup pass from me; nevertheless, not as I will, but as you will.'"

Prayer: 'I am the servant of the Lord; <u>let it be to me according to Your word</u>.' Amen.

(Mary's cousin Elizabeth speaking)
"Blessed is she who believed
that there would be a fulfillment
of what was spoken to her from the Lord."

Luke 1:45

the *expectancy* of Mary

expectancy: anticipatory belief or desire

Many days passed between "May it be to me" (Luke 1:38) and "Unto us a child is born" (Luke 2:11). Approximately 280 days. Days of sweating in the heat of the Middle Eastern desert. Days of puffy face and ankles. Days of jouncing along on the back of a camel with a 7lb embryo and swollen breasts.

Let us not over-spiritualize Mary's pregnancy. When we do, we take the sacred, beautiful ordinariness out of her faith.

'Well, *I'm* not as spiritual as Mary because *I'm* just so blah, so ordinary, so tired,' you say to yourself. Yes, my friend, you are indeed blah, ordinary, and tired. Congratulations. But it is usually right there in the blah, in the ordinary, in the tiredness where God's Spirit specializes in beautiful, sacred work.

'But *I'm* not assigned to such a spiritual task as Mary, carrying the holy Son of God around in my body,' you say. Here's where you are wrong, my friend: you *are* carrying the very Spirit of God around in your body! And you have been given the *extremely* spiritual task of spreading love to the people around you!

The ever-present challenge for me when I'm buried in the blah of the laundry - dirty dishes - school fundraisers - homework - diapering - yardwork is, first, to *bring myself to an awareness of God's work in my life*, and, second, to *believe that that work is deeply spiritual and profoundly significant*.

Instead of "Why won't the laundry ever *end*, Lord!?" I must ask, "What do you have for me today, Lord? Where are You at work invisibly, just below the surface?"

Instead of "I'm so ordinary; how could God ever use me for anything spectacular?" I must learn to pray, "Lord, I am particularly, especially, spectacularly ordinary! I expect You to use me!" Take a few moments to meditate on the following. Both lean forward onto the toes of expectancy.

> Psalm 5:3 In the morning, LORD, you hear my voice; in the morning I lay my requests before you and wait *expectantly.*

> Philippians 1:6 And *I am sure of this*, that he who began a good work in you will bring it to completion at the day of Jesus Christ.

If God uses ordinary people in ordinary circumstances, if He is resolved to work in me for good, my whole life should be pregnant with expectation.

Prayer: <u>Help me to see Your</u> ever-present, significant, miraculous <u>work in my life, Lord</u>, even when I'm buried in dirty laundry – or clean laundry, for that matter.

*"Mary had been betrothed to Joseph,
before they came together she was found to be
with child... And Joseph, being a just man
and unwilling to put her to shame, resolved to
divorce her quietly."*

Matthew 1:18-19

Joseph's *questioning*

I can only imagine the questions swirling in Joseph's head as he faced the prospect of marrying an, apparently, unfaithful fiancé and becoming an insta-stepdad: *Is Mary's story of the angel and her supernatural conception really true? What will this special child be like? Will I be a good father? Will I love him enough? Am I up to the challenge?*

In my own way, I ask these kinds of questions all of the time when a circumstance in my life seems daunting: *What is really true? What will the future hold? Will I have what I need? Will I be enough?*

And then...I come to the same conclusion Joseph did: *Nope. Not going to do it. Can't. Won't.*

Matthew 1:20-21, 24 "But as he considered these things, an angel of the Lord appeared to him in a dream, saying, '...do not fear to take Mary as your wife, for that which is conceived in her is from the Holy Spirit. She will bear a son, and you shall call his name Jesus, for he will save his people from their sins.' ...When Joseph woke, he did as the angel of the Lord commanded."

And then...God let Joseph in on the broader Story of all stories that was now beginning a new level of fulfillment: the mission of the salvation (the *healing, preserving, rescuing*) of all people. God was beckoning Joseph to take part, to let His Story engulf his story.

And so...Joseph moved forward confidently. Not because his questions were all answered. Not because he knew he'd never mess up, never have regrets. But because his story mattered far less than His Story.

Prayer: Sometimes, Lord, I feel like all I have in my life are questions with no answers. Go *with me*. <u>Paint over my story with the broad brush of Your Story.</u>

26

*"...you will conceive in your womb and bear
a son... And Mary said to the angel 'How will
this be, since I am a virgin?' ...'My soul magnifies the Lord, and my spirit rejoices in God
my Savior, for he has looked on the humble
estate of his servant. For behold, from now on
all generations will call me blessed..."*

Luke 1:31, 34, 46-48

the *rejoicing* of Mary

When the angel left, Mary must have thought, '*No one's ever going to believe this.*' I'm sure she was partially right.

Upon the announcement to family and friends about their – ahem – unexpected impending arrival and their it's-not-what-it-looks-like-and-Mary-is-still-a-virgin-we-swear! speech, I'm sure Mary & Joseph were met with many an eye roll and disbelieving glance. In defense of their family and friends: how could they be made to understand? *Right*, an <u>angel</u> told you this. I'm sure there were some people in Mary & Joseph's hometown who never believed their story.

29

We've all faced before the reality of being misunderstood.

In moments of feeling especially misunderstood,
(after complaining about it to anyone who will
listen) I've heard God say, in the quietness of
my heart: "Are you willing to be misunderstood
for My sake? Will you relinquish your 'right' for
others to think well of you?"

I must learn to pray, with Mary, "They may
misunderstand me now – they certainly don't
see this circumstance [premarital pregnancy]
as a blessing! But, someday they won't just understand; they'll call me 'blessed!'" And then
she was joyful in being known and understood
by God.

How are you feeling misunderstood? Try telling
God about it. He certainly understands about
being misunderstood. (He gets misunderstood
a lot.)

Prayer: Help me to find joy when I feel lost in
the misunderstanding of others. <u>Turn my feeling sorry for myself into happy praise</u>.

"And she gave birth to her firstborn son and wrapped him in swaddling cloths and laid him in a manger, because there was no place for them in the inn."

Luke 2:7

the *helpless, dependent childlikeness* of Jesus

Jesus: the very Son of God, who, just moments ago was ruling and reigning with Father God, put His head through a birth canal.

Jesus: the very One who holds the molecules of the world together by His Word, confined Himself to atoms, molecules, cells, tissue, organs.

Jesus: one of the few who were actually present at the drawing board to design the human body from scratch, reduced Himself to blood, nerves, muscle, bone, skin.

33

Jesus: the perfect, holy, pure God, entered into the earthy realm of excrement, puke, and pus.

Jesus: the eternal spirit, entered the temporal world of disease, decay, and death.

Jesus: all-knowing, all-wise, wore some kind of diaper.

He let Himself have needs. He let Himself have a mama. He let people see Him as less than He was.

And I have trouble letting someone help me – even when it's obvious that I *really* need it. I have trouble accepting others' generosity toward me. I have trouble letting people think that I'm even slightly less intelligent, less independently wealthy, or less capable than I think I am.

Prayer: Remind me of my utter helplessness and dependency on You, my Creator and my Parent. Remind me that I could always be thanking You for all of the air and water You gave me for Christmas. Then help me to let You help me (perhaps through others) as the one True Source of all that I need.

"And all who heard it wondered..."

Luke 2:18

the *wonder* of those who heard

wonder: to see God's creative, beautiful work (whether natural or supernatural) and to enjoy, be in awe, marvel

I studied Genetics & Cell Biology in college. I remember being flabbergasted at how many times my textbooks used the word "phenomenon." It was their go-to, catch-all word to describe a scientifically observed process, structure, or organism for which there was no "reasonable" explanation. I loved it. These textbook authors had found the supernatural in the natural and they didn't know what to call it. I made it into a sacred ritual: every time I saw that word, I used it as an opportunity to wonder at God's design scattered throughout our natural world.

I have perhaps never before witnessed human

beings engage in such wonder as I have recently, watching my two preschool boys marvel at their newborn baby brother. Every time the babe says "goo," belches, or – heaven, help us! – smiles at them, a wonder-fest breaks out. "Mom, did you hear that *big* burp!?" "Mom! He *smiled*! He likes me." It is a beautiful thing, and it never gets old. They see the phenomenal in the natural mannerisms of a baby boy, and they can't help but draw the attention of all within earshot.

Here are a few other ways we make room for wonder in our ordinary home, amongst our ordinary days:

> • When someone gets hurt: "Ouch! I'm sorry you scraped your knee. It's a good thing God made your body to do its best to heal itself! Isn't that amazing? In just a few days we won't even be able to see that scrape anymore."

> • As we harvest our summer garden: "Wow! Look at that huge cucumber! It was barely even there yesterday! All we did was plant those little plants and God gives them the sun, soil, and water they need to grow – all while we eat popsicles and pick our noses."

- Oh, one more thing: We watch "Smarter Every Day" online. If you haven't already discovered this, you're so welcome.

Prayer: <u>Fill my heart with wonder toward You, God</u>, as I look for Your fingerprints everywhere I go.

*"When the wise men saw the star,
they rejoiced exceedingly with great joy."*

Matthew 2:10

the *exceedingly great joy*
of the wise men

Who are the smartest people you know? University professors? Scientific researchers? Nuclear physicists? People with lots of letters after their names?

Smart people dance when nerdy things happen. Intellectuals celebrate when they discover something profound, something meaningful, or something that is breakthrough in their field. And these wise men, these brilliant people, when they saw the star they'd trekked all over the greater Middle Eastern continent to follow, apparently danced around like goofballs. They'd discovered something they knew made a difference in the world.

In America today, you might hear that Jesus is for uneducated, needy, unenlightened people. You might hear that following Jesus is a crutch for weak people who need such nonsense. I can assure you, dear friend, that that simply is not true. Yes, there are a lot of brilliant people who identify as atheists. But there are also a lot of brilliant people who have let Jesus take over their lives. If you don't believe me, look up Blaise Pascal, Adrian of Canterbury, or Dorothy Sayers, to name a few.

The wise men make an essential appearance in our story to show that Jesus is not just for uneducated shepherds, teenage virgins, and heavenly beings. This newborn Jesus was also very much for brilliant people - the kind of people who are often squeamish around babies.

Prayer: <u>Jesus, You are for everybody.</u> I'm not choosing intellectual inferiority just because I'm choosing You.

"And it had been revealed to Simeon by the Holy Spirit that he would not see death before he had seen the Lord's Christ.. [Simeon speaking] *"Lord, now you are letting your servant depart in peace, according to your word; for my eyes have seen your salvation..."*

Luke 2:26, 29-30

the *peace* of Simeon

What are you hoping for your life? I don't know about you, but - whether consciously or subconsciously - I ask myself this question all the time. I have lots of hopes and dreams and wishes and expectations and plans. Probably too many. The more you have, the more easily they may get shattered, I suppose.

Here we learn from our old friend Simeon a much better question: *What is God hoping for your life?*

Obviously, at some point, God had given Simeon a call on his life: that he would see *God's sal-*

45

vation. We don't know if it had been a dream, a vision, or this phrase pressed indelibly upon his heart. We don't know if some days he doubted that he had actually heard God correctly. We don't know if some days he felt discontented, wondering if it ever really would happen. But, we know that one day, Simeon went to the Temple, as he always did. And that day, *there He was*: the salvation; the baby Savior. All of Simeon's waiting and hoping and wishing flooded with peace.

When I listen for God's call on my life, and then let it replace or refocus whatever plans I had for my life, I can restfully wait (not work-work-work) and be at *peace* (not an anxious mess) with however and whenever He brings that call to its fulfillment.

Prayer: <u>Lord, what call do you have on my life?</u> (Listen, letting Him impress something on your heart.) I'll take it! And I'll actively wait on You as you bring it to my life.

"Then Herod, when he saw that he had been tricked by the wise men, became furious, and he sent and killed all the male children in Bethlehem and in all that region who were two years old or under..."

Matthew 2:16

the *fury* of King Herod

This is atrocious. As I write, I am rocking my well-under-two-year-old male child on one arm. I cannot fathom the reality of a governmental power rushing into my home, unannounced, wrenching my babe from my arms, and murdering him as I watch with my own eyes – and having absolutely no recourse.

Only deep-seated anger borne out of insecurity, self-preservation, and a hunger for power could cause a person to order the murder of thousands of babes. Only a chicken$h1t coward could order such genocide without having to execute any of it himself.

It is easy to be baffled by Herod's murderous appetite to remain in power. But, if I'm honest, there are moments when I rage just like Herod. I can't help but see part of my heart reflected here. I may not be ready to murder babies in the physical sense, but when, in His Sermon on the Mount (Matthew 5-7), Jesus redefined a murderer as anyone with anger in his or her heart toward another person, I find myself well within the range of homicide.

I am queen of my life, thank you very much, and I am absolutely enraged whenever some other potential ruler – God or man – gives me constructive feedback or attempts to show me how I'm not being the best good queen to myself or others.

The longer I follow Jesus, the more often this Good King Jesus seems to sweep into what I consider to be *my* jurisdiction, seeking to rule more and more of my life. Sometimes I resist him -- furiously, loudly, shaking my fist. Sometimes I quietly consent on the outside, though months or years later I find myself still stoking a quiet, smoldering fury. And sometimes, by God's Grace I can pray this instead:

Prayer: Help me to see that, <u>Jesus, You are the best good King</u>. Give me the inner strength to let You take over every corner of my heart, soul, mind, and strength.

"A voice was heard in Ramah,
weeping and loud lamentation,
Rachel weeping for her children;
she refused to be comforted,
because they are no more."

Matthew 2:18

the *weeping* of the women
who lost their children

Have you ever felt this kind of pain: deep, searing, only-tears pain with not a thing to smile about?

I have had a taste of this kind of pain before. On my worst days, I wanted not to believe in God because it was harder to believe that He was there and not bailing me out of the pain. It was sort of like Christian atheism. On my best days, I could say - with a tiny seed of hope - 'God is not who I thought He was. And He is doing a deep work to change the way I think about Him."

I was fortunate to have a few family and friends who did two essential things on my behalf. First, they truly prayed for me. It wasn't their exact right words in prayer that I needed; it was just their lifting me up to the One who knew what I needed and could do something about it. Second, they held out hope for me when I couldn't hold out hope for myself.

I have two questions for you to consider today:

> • Who in your faith community can you ask to have hope in your stead when you have none?

> • Who among your family or friends is in a situation where they are fresh out of hope and need you to hold out hope on their behalf?

Prayer: Oh God! Rescue my heart when it feels the kind of hurt that makes it only weep. <u>Give me patient, quiet compassion</u> when I find others who feel pain and hopelessness.

*"But Mary treasured up all these things,
pondering them in her heart."*

Luke 2:19

the *treasureful pondering*
of Mary

Mary enjoyed the moment. She soaked it all in. She looked around her - even at the chaos of a newborn babe's feeding needs and a temporary home full of barnyard animals - and actually savored it, loved it, enjoyed it.

I'm afraid we all have some version of messing up our present moment. Some of us wallow in the guilt, shame, and regret of the past. Others of us are obsessed with achieving perfection in the present. Still others of us hurtle our hearts toward the optimistic "someday" of the future.

Whatever poison we choose, our present moment - burgeoning with its own love, joy, gratitude - is lost to us and to those around us.

What distracts you most from your present moment: past, present, or future (as described above)? What do you need to let go of in order to make room in your present moments for treasureful pondering?

How does God want to change your way of thinking so that you can be more present (*engaged, actually listening, mindful of others, sensitive to the voice of God*) in the present? Ask Him.

Prayer: Oh God, don't let the chaotic frenzy of my life fill up every last corner of my mind and heart! Help me to save room for You in habitual, treasureful pondering.

[Gabriel, speaking to Mary]
"Greetings, O favored one, the Lord is with you! ...You have found favor with God."

[angelic choir, speaking of all mankind]
"Glory to God in the highest, and on earth peace among those with whom he is pleased!"

[Luke, writing about Jesus]
"the child grew and became strong, filled with wisdom. And the favor of God was upon him."

Luke 1:28, 30; 2:14, 40

the *favor* of God

favor of God: good-will, good-pleasure, satisfac-
tion, happiness, delight; wanting the best good
for another person; wanting another person to
become the best person he/she was created to be!

I have a question for you: How does God feel about you? Honestly. What do you think runs through His mind when He hears your name?

I must confess: if you were to ask me that question, my first thought would not usually be "favor." More likely, my answer would be something along the lines of "anger," "disap-pointment," "ambivalence / too busy," or "dis-belief / frustration [that I can't seem to get any-thing right]."

It is such a challenge for me to believe that the

favor of God is on me; to believe that He enjoys me, invests in me, and wants my best good.

I can't help but wonder how my life would change if I could live securely, in full awareness of His favor. Hmmm... I think I'd have a humble confidence, secure in who I am right now and yet still moving forward to become all He created me to be. I think I'd feel free to "open the fridge" in His kingdom the way I am still allowed to do at my parents' home. I think I'd be able to be my authentic, needy, broken self in front of Him. And I think that I'd start to see and love others with a renewed appreciation for how He made them.

Prayer: You know everything about me. Yikes. And, yet, <u>You</u> still <u>love being around me</u>, You find me as a worthy place to invest Your resources, and You long for the best good to come to my life. Help me to know and live out of that.

Book 2

Passions of Christ's Death

.

Introduction
Passions of Christ's Death

L ent is the liturgical season that begins
on Ash Wednesday and proceeds until
Holy / Black Saturday. In the liturgical
calendar, Ash Wednesday is calculated as the
forty-sixth day previous to Easter. Forty days
are planned for fasting, skipping six Sundays
because they are feasting days rather than fasting days, mirroring Jesus' forty days of fasting
in the wilderness. The Council of Nicea in 325
AD ordained Easter as a moveable feast: it is
always the Sunday after the paschal full moon
(the full moon that falls on or after the spring
equinox). Therefore, Easter is always the first
Sunday after the first full moon that falls on or
after March 21.

The twelve devotional readings that follow were written as spiritual fodder for the Lenten season. Therefore, begin reading The Passions of Christ's Death on Ash Wednesday, the first day of Lent, and read one passion every 3-4 days. Or, alternately, wait to start reading on the fifth Sunday of Lent and read one passion every day for the last twelve days before Good Friday.

The arrangement of the twelve passions here is chronological, but otherwise arbitrary. Each is a stand-alone thought, and so they may be experienced in any order one chooses. Proceed numerically, from 1 to 12, if you must. Or, live on the edge: Choose the passion that best reflects the kind of day you're having, or the passion that best describes the kind of day you wish you were having.

Each of the twelve readings magnifies one of the many various passions surrounding Jesus' death, in order to make the story feel more real, more human, and more relevant for today. I pray that each of us would find more of ourselves in the lives of the ordinary people who stood in the garden, in the courtroom, and at the foot of the cross. And, above all else, I pray that together we would be drawn to more devotedly love that Young Man on the crucifix.

As we stare into the emotive, physical, and instinctive responses of these one dozen first century Jesus-followers, let us also take a hard look into our own interior lives. Let us not miss the opportunity to ask ourselves: What does it mean for our lives today that we share in the death of Christ? And do we have the guts to be completely honest in prayer: "My God, my God! Why have You forsaken me?"?

Then Simon Peter, having a sword,
drew it and struck the high priest's servant
and cut off his right ear. (The servant's name
was Malchus.) So Jesus said to Peter,
"Put your sword into its sheath; shall I not
drink the cup that the Father has given me?"

John 18:10-11

(Jesus immediately healed Malchus's ear -
Luke 22:51 - so don't worry about him.)

the *vehemence* of Peter

I'm sure you've known someone like Peter, whether personally or just in the news. Peter was one of those unique people who seemed to ooze with natural feistiness, someone whose emotions erupted more easily than most, someone who was prone to crankiness when things didn't go his way.

Trust me; I know. People like Peter can be exhausting and annoying! Their unfettered energy and irrational anger are just sometimes *too much*!

But we need them. We need them to wake us up to invisible injustice and oppression. We need

71

their energy to help us take action when we are more prone to crawling into the fetal position and letting passivity have a field day.

And I am concerned that our western world is largely unequipped to handle such humans. We prefer to shush them, to judge them, and then to medicate them.

Jesus' responds differently to Peter's vehemence. First, Jesus firmly and unequivocally put an end to Peter's knee-jerk violence: "Put your sword into its sheath." Jesus put an end to the *way* Peter expressed his feelings, but not to the *strength of feeling* itself.

We need harmony and diplomacy, patience and balance in this war-torn world. But in this dishonestly-nice world we also need criticism and honesty, intolerance of injustice. We need to uphold peace-making *alongside* Peter's challenging the status quo. We ought to strive for understanding and amicable talk *as we also* strive for heated-debate and seething anger at the forces that keep people in all kinds of chains.

I fear, friends, that sometimes we accidentally castrate people like Peter, simply because they make us feel uncomfortable. We silence the truth they bring simply because it brings us discomfort.

While Peter's vehemence was undoubtedly the thing that most got him into trouble, it was arguably one of the main character qualities for which Jesus chose him – first to be one of His Twelve learner-followers and then to give leadership to the disciples after He was gone. Interestingly, two other of Jesus' chosen disciples possessed a similar personality bent; He nicknamed them 'Sons of Thunder' – and He wasn't being ironic!

Therefore, if you are a person with an ever-simmering fire in your belly, please: Go! Run! Take the lead! Work for necessary change! Challenge the status quo! We need your devotion, commitment, and depth of feeling to make us better people and the world a better place. Direct your vehemence most intently toward the rottenness you see in the powers (not people) that govern this world and in your own sin diseases. But *also*: listen heartily to Jesus' "Put your sword into its sheath;" remain humble and meek in letting Jesus turn your outrage into self-accepting, others-respecting Love.

If you are a person whose personality is more naturally even-keel, give the Peters around you the gift of some nonjudgmental space! Pray for them. Do your utmost to honor the unfettered passions of the vehement people in your life; be patient with them as they learn to spill their beautiful rage into the world in the form Love for God and others. And let them get you riled up a bit when it is appropriate!

Prayer: <u>Father, mature and wisen-up our vehemence</u>; let it lovingly proclaim the passion-filled Way of Jesus.

Then Jesus said to them, "You will all fall away because of me this night..."
Peter answered him, "Though they all fall away because of you, I will never fall away."
Jesus said to him, "Truly, I tell you, this very night, before the rooster crows, you will deny me three times." Peter said to him, "Even if I must die with you, I will not deny you!"

Matthew 26:31-35

Peter's *denial* of his denial

Peter is remembered far and wide for his denial of Jesus, often with scorn. But what frightens me most, and what I think ought to make us most wary, is not his denial. It is his emphatic, insistent denial of his *potential* to deny Jesus.

In his denial of his denial, Peter ultimately disregarded his need for Jesus. He essentially rejected the Gospel of Jesus. The Good News in its fullness is: all wrongdoing is possible, yes, even a *propensity*, for all; *yet* right-standing and even intimate relationship with God is possible by grace through faith in *Him*. In his denial, Peter rigorously denied the indispensable first half of that Good News.

Peter seriously argued with Jesus, in front of everyone.

J: "You all are going to abandon me."

P: "*They* might, Jesus, but not me."

J: "Yes even you will, Peter."

P: "Nope! Not *me*. Never. Ever ever."

J: "Peter, listen! Tonight, in just a few hours, you will."

P: (plugging his ears) "No way, José! La-lee-la! I can't hear you; must not be true! Nope nope nope."

And then the stakes were raised. Then the circumstances got much more dark and difficult. Then Peter's hero and best friend became public enemy number one.

And Peter did the exact thing he *knew* he would *never* do.

Aren't we the same? When we say, even only to ourselves, 'I would *never* do that [slight or selfish or atrocious] thing!' we misunderstand our proclivity to have our own way, to maintain our comforts, to keep up appearances. When we say, 'I can't believe that person *did* that! I've never done *any*thing like *that*!' we misjudge our own hearts. In fact, it is very probable that in just the past week or in just the next month we have done or will indeed do something very much like *that thing*, whatever it might be.

Even if we never actually *deny* Jesus in word or deed – whatever that means - we show that we are wrong-thinking if we insist that we could never do such a thing. We reject the vital first half of the Gospel of Jesus when we hide from our own egos our potential to do or say or be wrong.

Prayer: <u>Lord, destroy the prideful, self-righteous parts of my heart</u> that say, "I'd *never* do such-and-such." Thank You for the Good News that even though I do such-and-such all the time, You rescue me.

79

"'My soul is very sorrowful, even to death...'
And going a little farther he fell on his face
and prayed, 'My Father, if it be possible, let
this cup pass from me; nevertheless, not as I
will but as you will.'"

Matthew 26:38-39

Jesus'
'Let this cup pass'

Obeying God is hard – it even was for Jesus. Obedience is not always *easy joy*. Our first instinct is often to say, "Pass."

Isn't that comforting - to have the empathy of Jesus in the places where obedience is or has been altogether undesirable for you?

When it comes to obeying God, you know that you always have the option just to say, "Pass" don't you? You do not *have* to obey Jesus. You can always quit. In fact, all of us quit at some point in some capacity. Some of us "pass" for a moment; some for a season; some for a lifetime.

Some of us finally quit because we were actually mostly just faking it all along. Some of us quit out of sheer boredom. But I'm afraid that the time when most of us take a "pass" is when it gets hard -- when we sense Him asking us to do something that we just plain don't want to do.

Jesus could have said, "Pass." Basically, here, that's exactly what He said. "Let this cup pass, please?" Then He looked up through tears into the olive trees and pressed His face to the dewy ground and re-phrased, "Unless this is the only Way. Then, I'm still in. Not as I will but as you will."

When we are witness to the faithful obedience of Jesus and other humans, especially through difficulty and pain, we find that we can trust God as we follow Him through our own grievous obediences. We find courage to face the day ahead, rather than saying, "Pass."

The image of the cup in the Bible is used in two ways. In many instances, it refers to the cup of God's wrath. In the other instances, the cup is a picture of feasting, of joy, of "Cheers! Salud! Skål! Gan bei! Kanpai! Na zdravje!"

Jesus gulped down the cup of God's wrath so that we needn't drink of it. Then, when He invites us to drink the cups of difficult obedience (of loving those who are hard to love, of generosity that costs us dearly, of self-sacrifice in order to bless others), we participate *with Him* in saying to God, "Thy will be done," looking with hope toward the day when we will say altogether, "Cheers!"

Prayer: <u>Father, turn my "Pass" into "Thy will be done" now and "Cheers!" later</u>.

And the high priest stood up and said, "Have you no answer to make? What is it that these men testify against you?" But Jesus remained silent. And the high priest said to him, "I adjure you by the living God, tell us if you are the Christ, the Son of God."

Matthew 26:62-63

Jesus' *silence*

Lambs are silent when they go to slaughter because they're ignorant. They are none-the-wiser about what is about to happen to them. Jesus was not ignorant; He "[knew] all that would happen to him." (John 18:4)

I'll admit it: I get kind of frustrated with His silence here. 'C'mon, Jesus! What're you doing?? Speak UP! What's happening to you isn't fair! What are you doing? Don't be weak and passive, don't let injustice go unanswered!'

For Jesus, silence was not passivity, nor even inaction. Silence was loving, active submission to those who would not listen.

He silently accepted the injustice, so that He could loudly proclaim justice later. He lost this trial so that He could win the Trial of all trials – our being made right with God. He was silent now so that later He could resoundingly tell Satan, "It is finished!"

It takes an incredibly patient person, deeply devoted to a greater calling than quick-fix, present-moment justice to remain silent as Jesus did. It takes an incredibly large view, deeply committed to self-sacrificing Love to remain silent as Jesus did.

You're quiet – at least in your heart – when you have nothing to prove, nothing to defend, nothing to justify.

Prayer: <u>Weld me to You, Lord Jesus; help me to see the big picture</u> so that I have no need to prove, to defend, or to justify myself and others.

But they [the chief priests and the crowds] *were urgent, saying, "He stirs up the people, teaching throughout all Judea, from Galilee even to this place..." The chief priests and the scribes stood by, vehemently accusing him.*

Luke 23:5, 10

(See also: Matthew 27:62-66; 28:12)

the *urgent cacophony* of the religious leaders

The religious leaders had been deliberating over how to get Jesus killed for quite some time. Years, in fact.

And now, in the courtroom, with their urgently cacophonic verbal-spew, they stand in striking dissimilarity to the silence of Jesus. They filled the air with many words: false accusations; calls for Jesus to defend Himself; mockery. Can you feel in your gut the desperation and the revengeful exhilaration that must have raged in theirs?

These religious leaders were distraught, rushing to justify (through a trial) the injustice (of putting to death an innocent man) in order to experience the vindictive relief of having Him dead already! So, in an irony of all ironies, they jury-rigged a hasty, illegal trial in order to make legal His crucifixion. They unjustly justified themselves.

By both Jewish and Roman standards, the trial of Jesus was entirely out of order. From the time of day it was conducted to the manner of the malicious witnesses, suffice it to say, if appealed, Jesus certainly would have won.

Only when He was dead, they conjectured, would they finally be able to sleep at night.

So in the wee hours of Friday morning, they tried Him. Then, they killed Him.

But then, Friday night, they still couldn't sleep. The words of that wretched imposter, 'After three days I will rise,' had been ringing in their ears all night while they tossed and turned. I can hear their wives, "Honey, He's *dead*! You finally got what you wanted. Now *please* just go to sleep."

Saturday morning, they reconvened in Pilate's court. They implored Pilate to doubly-secure the tomb: by sealing the stone and guarding it with soldiers. After all, no one – neither Jew nor Roman – could endure the possibility that His disciples would attempt a break-in to steal the body, passing it off as a resurrection.

I wonder how they slept on Saturday night. I wonder if they let themselves entertain the possibility of a resurrection-rescue from <u>inside</u> the tomb. There was no way to secure a tomb from something like that. I can hear their wives again, "Honey, oh-my-Yahweh, don't be ridiculous. *That kind of stuff doesn't happen*. GO to *sleep*!"

What issues, what people cause you to fill the air with dire soliloquies? What fears, what anxieties, what longings for vindication make you lose sleep? Of who or what circumstance are you hasty to rid yourself? Who or what do you often put to an unfairly speedy trial? What if embracing that difficult person or situation might *actually* be God's path of salvation for you? How might God be longing to resurrect you from inside out? How might God's Way of resurrection be through – rather than in spite of – the person or circumstance you'd rather quell?

For the next week, practice a cessation of all

anguish, worry, and urgent talk you heap toward ridding yourself of this wretched person or thing. Ask God to show you, instead, how quiet self-sacrifice can triumph over swift guillotine.

Prayer: Quiet my accusations; quiet my blaming; quiet my vindictiveness; quiet my self-centered angst. Help me see Your salvation in unexpected places, from the inside out.

For [Pilate] *perceived that it was out of envy that the chief priests had delivered* [Jesus] *up.*

Mark 15:10

the *envy*
of the religious leaders

Wait. We've seen this kind of envy before. We saw it when Jesus was born: an envious, power-hungry leader (Herod) sought to kill infant Jesus before He could take the throne. Herod wanted to *be* Him – or at least to be king forever, so... he tried to kill Him in a regional toddler-genocide. And now again: These religious leaders wanted to *be* Him, so... they plotted and, finally, killed Him.

Envy is one of those disgustingly perverted, twisted ways of thinking: You want to be them so much so that it makes you want to *utterly destroy* them?! There are so many qualities about them that you *like* and *want for yourself* that it drives you to *sabotage* them – even to death?!

But perhaps the most revolting thing about envy is the way in which it surreptitiously hides itself in self-pity and ambition; it is quite hard to detect, especially in oneself.

I know a woman who is especially envious. (She'd openly admit it to you if you asked – that's the only way I know.) She told me that she goes through life with an incredible sense of longing and a keen awareness of her flawedness in comparison with others. Yet, because of Jesus changing her heart day by day, God has begun to redeem her envy.

Her part in her salvation from envy is this: She regularly owns her envy, calling it what it is and mourning in her heart over its toxic desire to remove and destroy the people toward whom she directs it. Then – as a counteracting expression of non-envy – she publicly *praises* the person she envies. And it's working. She told me that her mind is being changed, that she really has begun to see the victory of others as a victory for herself and for the entire community of Jesus-followers. I was particularly fascinated to hear her talk about this growing transformation because, in fact, I would describe her as one of my friends who most sincerely *rejoices with me when I rejoice* and most deeply *weeps with me when I weep.* "That seems like the exact opposite of envy," I told her. "Ha!" she said. And then she proceeded to brag about Jesus changing her.

A person prone to envy transformed into a selfless champion of others? It appears that, even though they eventually succeeded in killing Him, the envy of Herod and the religious leaders did not have the final say over the Envy-Conqueror.

Prayer: <u>Where is envy lurking in my heart, Lord?</u> Show me! And be persistent at tearing it out, piece by piece.

So when Pilate saw that he was gaining noth-
ing, but rather that a riot was beginning, he
took water and washed his hands before the
crowd, saying, "I am innocent of this man's
blood; see to it yourselves."

Matthew 27:24

the *absolvence* of Pilate

Pilate wanted to wash his hands of Jesus' blood.

So he tried. He said, "I am innocent of this man's blood," and he made a ceremonial show of washing his hands of the entire situation.

But it didn't work. He was still culpable. Pilate was, indeed, Jesus' last line of judicial defense – his last chance to escape the cruel Cross.

Pilate wanted to wash his hands *of* Jesus' blood. He needed to wash his hands *with* Jesus' blood.

He wanted to absolve himself. And, that's just the thing: he couldn't. Only Jesus could absolve

Him. And He did. "Father, forgive them for they know not what they do," Jesus prayed from the cross for those – including Pilate – who were putting Him to death.

Oh, how I long to wash my hands of so many things! And, yet, I am not fully embracing the lostness of this earth and my part in it until I see that I am inescapably culpable. My placating; my stubbornness not to love the unlovely; my stinginess in believing that my resources are, indeed, all *mine*; my blindness that keeps me from seeing how I hurt the people around me... Father, forgive me. I know not what I do.

Prayer: <u>Thank You, Jesus, for washing me with Your blood.</u>

And all the people answered, "His blood be on us and on our children!"

Matthew 27:25

the *self-damning*
of the crowd

They got their wish.

But not in the way they might have expected. His blood would not be counted *against* them, nor "on them," nor condemning them. It would be made available *to* them, to be counted *for* them, washing "over them," cleansing their hearts.

This is the ever-beautiful thing about Jesus. As we give Him more and more of our lives and hearts, He continually takes what we think we *want* and gives us instead what it is that is really *best* for us. Sometimes those two things overlap. Oft times they don't.

I ask Him to remove my discomforts; instead He gives me His ever-renewing soul-comfort by His Spirit.

I ask Him to make my worries go away; He says to tell Him all about it - He'll trade me my burdens for a lightness of step.

I come to Him on behalf of a sick or hurting friend; He says, "I'm holding her in the palm of My very hand."

"I'm hungry for more," I complain; He says "I am your Bread of life. My will sustains you even better than food."

I ask Him for financial security; He shows me that any kind of security outside of rightness/friendship with Him is just a well-marketed myth.

I tell Him how tired my body is; He rests my soul.

I tell Him how hopeless I feel; He brings a new day.

I say that I'm lonely; even if a friend doesn't appear, He Himself buoys me up.

"I'm getting old," I say; "Yes, you are, my darling girl, but your inner self is being renewed day by day."

I wonder how many of those in the crowd on that early morning of the trial later became Jesus-followers. I wonder how many of them are saying now, alongside us: "I asked for His blood on my head; instead His blood washed my heart! To Him be all honor and praise!" Amen and amen!

Prayer: <u>Thank You, Jesus, that even my own blood is not on my head, because Your blood covers my heart.</u> Keep giving me what You know I need, even when it is not what I think I want.

And over his head they put the charge against him, which read, "This is Jesus, the King of the Jews." ...And those who passed by derided him, wagging their heads and saying, "...save yourself! If you are the Son of God, come down from the cross." So also the chief priests, with the scribes and elders, mocked him, saying, "He saved others; he cannot save himself. He is the King of Israel; let him come down now from the cross, and we will believe in him."

Matthew 27:37, 39-42

the *mockery* of strangers

It is the easiest thing in the world to mock someone you don't know, someone whose story you have not heard.

Jesus must have looked, in those wee hours of the morn, like a supreme idiot: mute, abandoned, exhausted, forlorn. If only they'd heard His whole story; if only they'd known Who He was, why He was silent, what Power He had at His fingertips, and with what self-control He resisted calling on that Power. If they'd only known, they would have *shut their mouths*.

We all do the mocking.

There is always someone we can find who looks, to us, remarkably like an idiot. Whether it is their clothing, their grammar, their driving, their appetite, their work ethic, their gender, their confusion about their gender, their emotional expression, their finances, their theology, their lack of theology...

And we all are the mocked.

We each have been, at some time or another, the recipient of another person's disdain, for any of the above reasons – and more.

If mockery slides off your tongue as easily as it does mine:
Look to Jesus.

He was, indeed, King of the Jews, though not in the way you'd expect a king. This King, who could have obliterated that caustic sign above His head with a trillion laser beams from the future, absorbed the sarcasm of the sign by leaving it there.

He was, indeed, the Son of God; but He proved it by staying on the cross. He could, indeed, have saved Himself; He showed His Power by resisting its use.

There was, in this Jesus, far more to His story than met the eye. Consider, too, that this must be true of the recipients of your mocking.

If you are or have been the object of judging and jeering, especially from the mouths of religious people, for what it's worth: I'm so sorry.

And: Look to Jesus.

Secure in Who He was, He could love them through their sarcasm. Sure of His Mission, He could ignore their guffaws. Confident of His future triumph, He could withstand their very temporary condescension.

Prayer: <u>Keep my eyes on You and Your cross, giving me compassion toward others and strength to endure the mockery life brings.</u>

those who had been with him...
mourned and wept

Mark 16:10

the *mourning* of intimates

Mustn't someone mourn at His death? Everyone else, it seems from the text, was mocking, reviling, full of derision, and scornfully sarcastic.

Everyone who didn't know Him wanted to kill Him.

Everyone who knew Him mourned, wept, lost it, lost themselves, or ran away shamefully in self-preservation.

I know full-well that it is quite looked down upon to speak ill of the dead. But for the sake of the living, you'll allow me this story?

A friend of mine once told me about attending the funeral of her grandfather, whom she had known as well as anyone knew him. The deceased was a religious and church-going gent, but in his old age he had become quite self-centered and stingy (rather than others-centered and generous, in the direction you would hope and expect a Jesus-follower would grow). My friend had suffered a fair degree of hurt at his inconsiderate ways; she regretted that she had not experienced toward him genuine filial love and tenderness. In hushed tones, she admitted that she was not at all distraught at his passing.

Well, her grandfather had been quite a visible figure in his small town, outspoken and well-recognized by many. At the funeral, many people came up to my friend and said, "Oh, wasn't he such a wonderful person?!" And, "Oh, won't he be missed!"

And during this emotionally laborious receiving line, she told me that all she could think of in response to these strangers was, "It is obvious to me that you did not know him." (She did not say this, of course, because she is much too kind a person to speak ill of the dead, as those uncouth persons would dare to do.) She simply smiled in silence.

Those who did not know him were sad to see him go.

Those who really knew him, his 'intimates,' did not mourn.

It was after this conversation about this man's funeral that it dawned on me that I want the opposite to be true of me. I do not give a fig whether strangers, people on the 'outskirts' of my life, are glad or sad to see me gone. But, I want to be <u>known</u> by my inner circle, my dearest intimates, in a way that will cause us to experience great endearment toward each other. Isn't this one way to describe what love *is*?

Those who were in the intimate circle of Jesus really knew Him, felt endeared to Him, really loved and liked Him. He was that kind of a Person. And, of course, they wept their hearts out at His death.

They didn't realize yet what we know Sunday would bring: Jesus alive. Death dead.

Prayer: <u>Father, how am I accidentally hiding from and hurting my intimates?</u> Let me be known and loved and free – at least to those closest to me.

113

*When the centurion and those who were with
him, keeping watch over Jesus,
saw the earthquake and what took place,
they were filled with awe and said,
"Truly this was the Son of God!"*

Matthew 27:54

*One of the criminals who were hanged railed
at him, saying, "Are you not the Christ? Save
yourself and us!" But the other rebuked him,
saying, "Do you not fear God, since you are
under the same sentence of condemnation? And
we indeed justly, for we are receiving the due
reward of our deeds; but this man has done
nothing wrong."*

Luke 23:39-43

the *awe* and *fear*
of strangers

For these two men, a Roman centurion and a criminal of Rome, Jesus' most vulnerable, hopeless-looking moment is the moment when His true identity registers:

Roman centurion: [*filled with awe*] "Truly this was the Son of God!"

Criminal of Rome: "Do you not fear God? ...this man has done nothing wrong."

These men had not known Jesus personally. They were strangers to Him.

I don't know about you, but Jesus hanging on the cross, dying a grotesque, brutal, shameful death seems to me to be a most unlikely time for a person find faith: to be *filled with awe*, to talk of "fearing God," and to proclaim his innocence. When God is bloodied and dying? When innocence has been indicted and sentenced and is in the midst of being publicly executed?

We 'unstrangers' to God tend to have a contrarily strong preference: to see God win. We prefer to acknowledge God when He is giving us success – in our churches, our jobs, finances, our families, our adventures, our talents. We prefer to give God 'awe' and 'fear' when we are privy to natural wonders (gorgeous sunsets), supernatural signs (physical healings), and heartwarming stories (puppies that just missed getting run over).

But these two men 'owned' God when God looked defeated. They acknowledged God's reality, His might, His goodness, when it appeared that God, in utter weakness, was definitely going to lose.

Will I say, "Truly He is God's Son!" when all my hard work turns up futile? Will I "fear God" when my fervent prayers are answered only

116

with His silence? Will I say, "This Man has done nothing wrong," when I receive a terminal diagnosis?

Perhaps these 'strangers' respected God in a more mature way than I. Perhaps their trust of God was more honest, since they still trusted Him when He appeared untrustworthy. Perhaps they loved God more deeply because they loved Him even when they weren't getting all their wishes granted.

Prayer: <u>Fill us with awe and trust in You, even when we can see only death, darkness, and the earth falling apart.</u>

And when evening had come, since it was the day of Preparation, that is, the day before the Sabbath, Joseph of Arimathea, a respected member of the council, who was also himself looking for the kingdom of God, took courage and went to Pilate and asked for the body of Jesus. [Joseph was a rich man and also a disciple of Jesus.] Pilate was surprised to hear that he should have already died. And summoning the centurion, he asked him whether he was already dead. And when he learned from the centurion that he was dead, he granted the corpse to Joseph. And Joseph bought a linen shroud, and taking him down, wrapped him in the linen shroud and laid him in [his own new] tomb that had been cut out of the rock. And he rolled a stone against the entrance of the tomb.

Mark 15:42-46
in combination with
Matthew 27:57-60

the *courageous, tender anonymity* of Joseph of Arimathea

J oseph the courageous.

Courage on behalf of a dead man.

Courage for the sake of someone who would (as far as he knew) never know it.

Courage – finally – in this story about a long line of religious and political *cowards* that led to the public, grotesque death of an innocent man.

Courage to ask for kindness and honor from a high-ranking governmental figure who had just shown a disgraceful display of cowardice.

Joseph of Arimathea represents the invisible, anonymous courage of many saints, then and now.

I'm not very good at this kind of courage. I'm better at the publicly celebrated, noticeable, tax-deductible kind of courage.

But this is the Jesus Way. Joseph of Arimathea risks his life by going to Pilate, and then he does the dirty, unglamorous, unreciprocate-able work of wrapping and entombing a dead body.

Are you taking risks, but wondering if they're making a difference? Are you doing things for people who can't reciprocate? Are you feeling utterly anonymous in your life or marriage or parenting or friendships or job or church? Congratulations! That is the Way of Jesus. Even Jesus was once that helpless dead person who let Himself need someone like you to serve him with courage and tenderness. He sees what you do in the quiet of your heart.

Prayer: <u>Jesus, teach me to serve You and the people around me</u> like Joseph served You and <u>like You serve me - every single day.</u> Courageously. Tenderly. Anonymously.

Book 3

Passions of Christ's Resurrection

Introduction
Passions of Christ's Resurrection

UnLent is the name I have begun to call the forty-or-so days between Jesus' resurrection and ascension. N. T. Wright was the first to point out to me how puny, how mundane, and how short-lived was our typical western observance of Jesus' resurrection.[1] And so in response to Wright's observation, dear reader, I submit to you an entire appendix of ideas for a more robust practicing of UnLent! (See Appendix III.)

The following twelve devotionals were written for the season of UnLent: the forty days between Easter Sunday and the Ascension. The best plan may be to begin reading on Easter Sunday - the first day of UnLent – reading 2-3 passions per week until completion.

The twelve UnLent devotionals are ordered chronologically as found in the four-storied accounts of Jesus' rising from the dead. However, they stand-alone and therefore may be experienced in any order one chooses. Perhaps you will do well to submit to the whim of your current emotions when you come to read, choosing then the passion that best describes the emotion that has enveloped most of your day, or choosing the passion of which you feel most in need.

Each reading takes a close look at one of the many varying emotional responses to Jesus' resurrection or post-resurrection appearance. A focus on emotion is intended to make the story feel more real, more human, and more relevant for today. My prayer is that each of us would find ourselves in the minds and hearts of these firsthand witnesses, and, above all else, that we would be drawn irretrievably to a more devout love for that Man who escaped even the Tomb.

As the resurrection passions surfaced one by one, I fairly expected that their overall tone would be elation, joy, and celebration. It did not take long for me to find that I was terribly wrong. It took even less time for me to find great comfort in that reality. After all, neither are elation, joy, and celebration *my* overall, constant tone during every day of every Un-Lenten season. Apparently I am not all that different from these resurrection eyewitnesses.

126

I do a fair enough job of adopting an appropriately sour mood for the 40 Lenten days. (*How else can one be when one is depriving one's body from its usual intake sugar, coffee, or treats?*) But hardly do I adopt – even for the brief 40 UnLenten days – the life-giving, life-bringing, life-receiving, whooping and hollering, lively emotional response that is borne from the truth of the Resurrection. Apparently I have much room to grow.

As we take time to glimpse the varying reactions of these one dozen first century Jesus-followers to an alive-again Jesus, let us not neglect to peer into our own interior lives. Let us ask ourselves: *What is my everyday posture toward the irrationally good news that "He is not here, but he has risen!"?*

[1] Wright, N. T. *Surprised by Hope.* pg 107, 257, 267-268.

So they departed quickly from the tomb with fear and great joy, and ran to tell his disciples.

Matthew 28:8

...they were alarmed... And they went out and fled from the tomb, for trembling and astonishment had seized them, and they said nothing to anyone, for they were afraid.

Mark 16:5, 8

While they were perplexed about this, behold, two men stood by them in dazzling apparel. And as they were frightened and bowed their faces to the ground, the men said to them, "Why do you seek the living among the dead?"

Luke 24:4-5

Jesus himself stood among them and said to them, "Peace be to you!" But they were startled and frightened and thought they saw a spirit.

Luke 24:36-37

the *fear*
of the men & women disciples

Of course they were scared. Jesus – the Man-God they'd come to know and love, the One in whom they'd come to Hope as Messiah – was definitely dead. And all that they thought they'd come to know about him and his Way had come to nothing along with him – how could it not? If he was God, if he was the Messiah who was poised to *rescue* the Jews, then certainly he would not have *died*. This was not at all the rescue they'd anticipated. It could not be.

Let us be clear: These male and female disciples of Jesus were experiencing that upending mix of surprise, joy, and terror that comes whenever one faces the undoing of something that

129

one had known, something about which one was positively sure. Therefore, when the physical Jesus made his abrupt reappearance in their gardens and living rooms, *all* of their previous dogmas about Jesus and about Death itself began to unravel. At a very interior level, many of their most foundational conclusions were thrust suddenly into the delicately vulnerable process of utter *undoing*.

I used to live under the basic assumption that God wanted me to have a happy, easy life. But that God contracted a terminal illness during some years when my life circumstances could be described as far less than cheery. My happiness quotient continued to spiral further and further downward as every day seemed to bring more bad news with no good news in sight. The mental disturbance of depression ensued – how could it not? – and it was enough to put that God out of his misery once and for all.

So be it. He needed to die. It was better for both of us.

God came back to life in my mind and heart, but when he did, he was different than the one who'd died. This new God still wanted my Good, but not in the perpetually smiley way I'd formerly thought, and definitely not at the cost of my inner strength of character.

This kind of undoing has happened to me a handful of times in my life. And every time, I'm scared to death. Fearful-as-I-watch-an-entirely-new-world-open-up-before-my-very-eyes-and-I-can't-control-it-and-my-life-will-never-be-the-same-after-this-and-I-must-let-go-of-something-about-which-I-was-absolutely-certain-or-at-least-I-thought-so-and-here-come-the-happy-horror-tears-but-I-can-feel-myself-getting-freer-and-freer-by-the-moment-so-this-must-be-the-path-of-Jesus! In those moments of self-discovery, there is simply no other way to be but absolutely, ecstatically terrified.

When is the last time, like these men and women disciples, that alarm, trembling, and astonishment *seized* you?

When is the last time that you allowed your resolute ideas – about God, about Death, about anything – be completely undone -- so undone that it felt like an unraveling in your own interior life? What notions about God and his Good Life, or about Death and its hells in this world still need undoing in your mind and heart?

What if letting some of our ideas crumble a bit would be to our ultimate benefit? What if letting go might lead us to a newer, more real kind of Freedom? What if finding surety in our own knowledge and dogmas is actually just another version of self-salvation? What if leadership of our lives is to come not from our theological convictions, but from a Person, from Jesus?

Prayer: <u>God: Let crumble my human-thoughts of you!</u> Then, in a blessed union of Fear and Joy, come back to life and show up at my kitchen table -- to my happy horror!

But on the first day of the week, at early dawn, they went to the tomb, taking the spices they had prepared. And they found the stone rolled away from the tomb, but when they went in they did not find the body of the Lord Jesus. While they were perplexed about this, behold, two men stood by them in dazzling apparel. And as they were frightened and bowed their faces to the ground, the men said to them, "Why do you seek the living among the dead? He is not here, but has risen."

Luke 24:1-6

the *poignant question* of the
two men in dazzling apparel:
"Why do you seek the living
among the dead?"

I love this question. It is so rude: These poor
women had seen Jesus die before their very
weeping eyes; what else were they to expect
other than to find him dead and entombed? Furthermore, they had come in love and honor to
do the beautiful, filthy job of caring for his dead
corpse; the angels need not be so patronizing:
These women were looking for the dead among
the dead.

I love this question. It is so to the point. It bursts
through the women's sad expectations with
happy news! It does not keep its glad tidings to
itself for a moment longer than it must: He is
alive! No longer does he lie, helpless and inert in

a cavern. He might be anywhere!, everywhere!, who knows? But he is certainly *not* here.

In what ways do I still seek the living among the dead?

I seek the living among the dead every time I:

> ...expect someone – anyone, really, myself included – to act precisely like I suppose that Jesus would act.

> ...long for legislated religion, for a "christian nation." That is not Life; it is only a perceived sense of safety for religious people.

> ...expect greedy governmental systems to prioritize and solve the world's social, economic, or political problems in the grace-filled, generous way Jesus would.

> ...look for the Good Life among the tombs of unwillingness to be changed myself.

> ...expect life-giving results from the same death-bearing habits and patterns in which I find myself stuck.

> ...allow unforgiveness to fester in my heart because the other person hasn't asked for my

forgiveness or isn't repentant enough for my standards.

...accept any form of verbal, physical, emotional, political, relational, or religious violence as a Jesus-ordained option in his kingdom where enemies are to be loved.

Let the seeking of the live Jesus begin! He may be anywhere; He may be everywhere! All we know is that he is not dead; He is not lying like a corpse in a tomb.

May we seek the living Jesus wherever He may be found. May we expect to find Him among the living, the life-giving, the enlivening. All eternal, ever-enlivening, ever-life-giving life is found in Him. Any and all signs of human flourishing are to His credit. May we see Him in any and all of the things, all of the people, all of the ideas that bring life-giving life to ourselves, to others, to our world.

I came that they may have life and have it abundantly. John 10:10

Prayer: Keep redefining my ideas of the Good Life, of eternal life, of abundant life. Help me to see You, the Life, everywhere I go. Help me to bring Life to the people around me.

Having said this, she turned around and saw Jesus standing, but she did not know that it was Jesus. Jesus said to her, 'Woman why are you weeping? Whom are you seeking?" Supposing him to be the gardener...

John 20:14-15

But the eyes [of the men on the Emmaus road] *were kept from recognizing him.*

Luke 24:16

Jesus'
hiddenness

The direct, word-by-word reading of Luke 24:16 in Greek is as follows: "[the] eyes of them were held [so as] not to know him." The verb "held" means to lay hold of, to obtain, to seize for control. We are left with the sense that God's Spirit was intentionally preventing these men from beholding-in-full the physical, spiritual identity of their cojourner.

As offensive as it may be to our Western sensibilities, the idea of concealment, hiddenness, and mystery is a very common one in the Story of Jesus. Not only does God sometimes covertly keep people from understanding who, what, or why, but at times Jesus overtly urges people not to share with others the Truths that they have understood! (John 20:14, John 21:4, Matthew 11:25-26, Luke 9:45, Luke 18:34, just to name a few)

In our modern age, where knowledge is presumed to belong to everyone, where the transparency of corporations and leadership is an entitlement of the masses, and where more free and immediately accessible information is always better, we can hardly wrap our little brains around such an evasive Jesus!

Furthermore, why in heaven's name would Jesus ever *keep* anyone from recognizing him? It's terrible for public relations, it seems like preferential treatment, it is morbidly dishonest, and it is counterintuitive to growing the kingdom business!

But then I look into the eyes of my elementary-school child, and I get it. I see in him my own inability to handle all truth all at once, and I understand. I can't handle All of God. My mind and heart are not yet ready to receive all of the Truth.

I prefer to think of myself as quite enlightened, quite awakened, and quite in-the-know. I prefer to view myself as one of God's trusted advisors,

140

as one who has earned the right to be entrusted with His inside scoop. I prefer to compare myself to all of the ignorant, narrow, and unenlightened people around me – when, instead, I need only compare myself to God.

I am a child standing before a Being who knows All. And in that All that He knows are found my unawareness, my ignorance, my immaturity, my pride – all of which justify and retain His hiddenness from me.

If He, without qualification, instantaneously transmitted all of His Truth and Grace and Reality of Who He Is into my brain like some kind of disgusting internet file, it would not be a gift; it would be a curse. Such insight (about myself, about God) would inevitably march my ego straight down the road toward pride, self-righteousness, and pomp. In addition, and perhaps most tragically, it would virtually rob me of any opportunity for growth in my inner life. The strengthening of one's inner character may be attained only through good and proper wrestling, and through the gradual dawning of recognition.

No! He is wise to take His time with us. It is for us to trust Him to reveal Himself in His own good time. It is for us to thank Him for humbly and appropriately hiding Himself from us, giving us only enough of Him to keep us sure enough while still delightfully wondering.

Isn't it frighteningly enchanting to wonder with anticipation: What am I being kept today from recognizing about Him? ...about myself? What preconceived notions about Him keep me from recognizing Him when He shows up in my life, right before my very eyes? What immaturities remain in my inner life with God which insist on His hiddenness?

Isn't it wondrous to think: Oh, what vast knowledge of Him remains in the vault for me to discover, pearl by pearl! What deep intricacies of my story and of who He made me to be still remain in their hiding places, waiting to be beheld at the proper time!

It is, indeed, a very breathtakingly good reality: that I will have millions of years after this Earth to explore the Hiddenness of Christ in me, I in Him.

What lovely truths await!

Prayer: <u>Mature me into the kind of person</u> who can handle more and more of Who You are, <u>who humbly receives, who loves to understand,</u>

<u>who courageously grows</u>. Give me patience and contentment as I wait for Your Spirit's dawning in my life, revealing to me the mystery of Truth and the lavishness of Grace.

And [Jesus] *said to them,*
"What is this conversation that you are hold-
ing with each other as you walk?"
And they stood still, looking sad.
Then one of them, named Cleopas, answered
him, "Are you the only visitor to Jerusalem who
does not know the things that have happened
there in these days?" And he said to them,
"What things?"

Luke 24:17-19

Cleopas & his friend
standing still, looking sad

I'm sure you've done it before: assumed that someone had already heard the bad news, inadvertently inferred something about it, and *then* learned that they had obviously not yet been told. I hate when I do that. Any sober familiarity that the news had finally attained in my own heart is instantaneously lost; it becomes unconscionably bad news all over again. We both stand still, looking sad.

"What is this conversation that you are holding with each other as you walk?" Jesus' question feigned naïveté; it stopped Cleopas and his friend in their tracks.

The two men exchanged diffident glances, their, "How do we tell him?" coalesced with, "Seriously? Have you been living under a rock?" Jesus' prolonged look of complete unenlighten-

145

ment bordered on conversational cruelty. *What in heaven's name was He doing?* (Besides, of course, being excruciatingly socially awkward.)

Jesus asked them again. "What things? I hadn't heard." This time, they launched cautiously into the story. Jesus made them say it again. He made them explain it again. He made them verbally process it again. Aloud. All of it.

You see, for Jesus, this Story was not at all sad. The death of an innocent, the dissolution of a vibrant ministry, the disenchantment of an entire people group was not at all a disappointment to Jesus. Instead, it was <u>exactly</u> what Jesus expected. What Cleopas and his friend saw as failure was actually victory in the kingdom of Jesus, where the greatest value is steadfast, overarching and undergirding Love-without-conditions. Love expected; Love championed. Even if it costs the King his life, his success, his popularity. A dastardly cost - paid with nary a second thought.

'How could a person hear this Story and then stand here looking <u>sad</u>?' Jesus thought. 'Maybe <u>this</u> time, perhaps in <u>this</u> retelling, they'll see it: that what they thought was a sad story is actually the most splendid upside down Story they've ever heard. Yes, please, friends, explain it to Me again.'

"Well, there was this amazing guy who we thought was from God and was going to solve all our problems. But then our spiritual guides indicted and executed him. Some women went to his tomb and they said his body was missing; they are still holding out hope that he's alive, but, well..."

We are always all making and telling stories: about ourselves, about our lives, about how the world occurs to our hearts. Our stories begin somewhere, silently, in the recesses of our subconscious, where they grow until they are birthed into our hearts and out of our mouths. Left to their own devices, they take the wide and easy path of self-centeredness, of doubt and despair, of loneliness and helplessness. They wind downstream to their only self-fulfilling conclusion: that our lives, our circumstances, our leaders really are *that* bad, and that we really are as under-appreciated or under-paid as we'd thought. We really *are* so much more generous, capable, informed, aware, and open-minded than everyone else! At this point, our stories spill out and into our lives with some version of the same age-old conclusion: *Poor me; I'm great.*

147

Unless. Unless we allow the Spirit of God to interrupt the process, to pluck our stories up out of our self-centered orientation, to listen to them, to make us listen to them again -- then, and only then, perhaps, a different and much more interesting conclusion awaits them. If we will honestly and open-heartedly tell our stories aloud to and before Jesus (that is, if we will honestly and open-heartedly *pray* our stories), we will unfetter in ourselves the potential to find the splendid kingdom Story hidden in each sad human story.

It is often our default to dwell on all of the ways "Jesus is dead" in our lives -- just look at our bum-luck, our vices, and our grievances toward God and humans alike! But, when we force ourselves to say aloud, "Jesus is dead," when we pray our sad stories to God and in front of other safe humans, we have the opportunity – if we are open to such a thing – to be transformed. After all, it is us, not our sad stories, which need the changing. When we pray our sad stories over again, there is a chance that our idea of sadness might just be turned upside down. Ungratefulness may blossom into gratitude and a holding out of hope that "Jesus is alive and well." Misfortune may turn to providence - that a greater accident was not had. Anger may dissolve into accepting forgiveness, as God has accepted and forgiven me.

Prayer: Give me the honest open-heartedness I need to pray my sad stories to and before You, Lord Jesus: my stories of disappointment, offense, and hardship. <u>Take as prayer the downers on my lips; transform them into the upward movement that turns my heart toward the God who is very much alive and well.</u>

*"...our chief priests and rulers delivered him
up to be condemned to death,
and crucified him. But we had hoped
that he was the one to redeem Israel..."*
*"O foolish ones, and slow of heart to believe
all that the prophets have spoken! Was it not
necessary that the Christ should suffer these
things and enter into his glory?"*

Luke 24:20-21, 25-26

the *'we had hoped'* of the men on the road to Emmaus

L et us begin with a little word lesson:

redeem: v. to release or set free, to restore to a rightful owner, to rescue from the power and possession of an alien possessor, to liberate, to deliver.

suffer: v. to pay a cost, to have pain, to prioritize inner strength of character over temporary comfort.

glory: n. good opinion, weight, renown, honor, splendor.

"We had hoped that he was the one to redeem Israel," they said. *But of course he wasn't the one*, they concluded. *He simply couldn't have been the one. Didn't you see how he suffered and died? Redeemers don't suffer and die. Redeemers don't let their ministries fall flat and then subsequently abandon their people.*

Or do they?

Jesus seemed to have very different ideas about the very nature of redemption and the means through which it is comes. "Was it not necessary that the Christ should *suffer* these things and enter into his *glory*?"

The pathway to *redemption* was necessarily through suffering, even for the Christ.

The pathway to *glory* was necessarily through suffering, even for the Christ.

When you think about it for a minute, it makes sense:
To redeem someone or something always cost someone something. That is to say, someone or something always suffers in order to bring about the freedom and restoration of the other.

To give glory to an old furniture piece costs

152

something.

The stripping off of old paint, the sanding, the repairing of a compromised spot, the hunting for period-appropriate hardware, the fresh coatings of stain and lacquer altogether cost one time, money, elbow grease, and the willingness to get one's hands filthy.

To redeem the land costs something.

Land preservation, maintenance, and cleanup cost money in labor, equipment, and energy. One must also suffer the foregone temptation to exploit the land in the name of the quick and mighty dollar.

Farmland sustainability costs farmers time, money, and patience. Soil must lay fallow some years, crops must be rotated for enrichment, careful tending must occur throughout.

To restore a relationship costs something.

A divorced woman grieves her husband's infidelity. After years of separation, he comes to himself. He resolves to go to the ends of the earth to regain her trust. She risks it all, puts forgiveness in practice, and marries him again.

153

Two brothers stubbornly refuse to speak; their fight had gone too far this time. One finally humbles himself to begin the conversation again. Even when rebuffed, he initiates friendship again, tossing his self preserving dignity to the wolves.

Jesus (*my paraphrase*): "Don't you know that suffering, pain, costly love, and self-sacrifice all the way to death are exactly what redemption looks like?! For what had you hoped: Violence? The only violence I came to wage is against your selfish and worldly passions. For what had you hoped: Confetti? This is not a Disneyland parade. For what had you hoped: That Good would passively seep its way into this world by osmosis? Yes, in the end Good will prevail, but it will do so only at an exorbitant cost to the God and the people who participate in its flow to every corner of the earth."

"I suppose that you were hoping for the right thing, that is, for redemption; it's just that your expectations for *what it would look like* and *how it would come* were morbidly upside down. And so you missed it; you watched redemption go by you without even knowing when it was right under your nose. Incidentally, you might not recognize glory if it visited you right outside your window."

154

"Yes, whatever it was that you were hoping for died when that Man, Jesus, died. But in that very moment, Hope itself came alive."

Prayer: <u>Jesus, let our dead hopes die, only to find Your Hope alive in its place.</u> Restore us so that we may be conduits of Your ongoing Redemption and Glory to our inner lives, to the people around us, to our cities, to our countries, to our world, and to our age.

...but they urged him strongly, saying,
"Stay with us, for it is toward evening and the
day is now far spent."

Luke 24:29

the *strong urging* of the men
on the road to Emmaus
for Jesus to stay

Who is your spiritual hero? Who is the sage in your life who you *know* prays a lot and who always seems to have just the right insight for every difficult situation? Don't you sometimes wish that that person would just come and live with you? If only you could have access to them every moment, *then* you'd be quite a spiritual person indeed!

My dad often quotes a comedienne who said, "I don't need a diet plan; I need someone to follow me around all day and take the cookie *out of my hand*!" I often find myself daydreaming about the same kind of passive spiritual mentorship. Just follow me around, Jesus, and slap my hand whenever I'm about to make the wrong decision or give in to a temptation. In middle school I was instructed to imagine Jesus constantly in the room with me, as if then my life would automatically change. In a few ways, it might. But there is no guarantee. And wouldn't it only be on the outside?

Yes, a spiritual sage living in our upstairs bedroom might keep our voices lower when we're angry and remind us to clear our internet history more regularly, but their mere presence cannot substitute for the interior work we must do in our own hearts if we are to grow up spiritually.

Spiritual growth is hard work. And it cannot be done for us. No one can do it on our behalf, not even Jesus. Only we can do it. It begins in the invisible chasms of our heart, soul, mind, and strength. Eventually, slowly, it seeps out of our spiritual pores in the shape of a changed and changing life.

If we are really to grow and mature, our spiritual hero must depart. Like the best Good Parent, she must let go of our hand; he must disappear so that we will take steps on our own.

God has given us the every day, in and out, oxygenating breath of His Spirit. In His view, this is the best thing for us. It is even better than His living in our every nook and cranny, wagging his forefinger to remind us not to eat too much cake, and raising his eyebrow to keep us from acting out our road rage.

Maybe this is what Jesus meant when he said previously: "Nevertheless, I tell you the truth: it is to your advantage that I go away, for if I do not go away, the Helper will not come to you. But if I go, I will send him to you. And when he comes, he will convict the world (*especially you*) concerning sin and righteousness and judgment..." John 16:7-8 (*italics*, mine)

Whenever a well-respected leader, a heroine, or a savant leaves their post in this world, another human or humans must rise to the *external* and *internal* challenges of carrying on the way and the mission.

Jesus left His post in part so that we would learn character on our own, for ourselves. Our spiritual muscles of perseverance, joy, self-control in suffering, gratitude, and Love simply cannot grow to their full potential if we continue to be carried around on piggyback.

Prayer: Stay with me, Jesus! But only stay for as long as it is for my best good. <u>Don't You dare let me live a vicarious spirituality</u>, immaturely relying on the insight and inner strength of others rather than on my very own.

They said to each other, "Did not our hearts burn within us while he talked to us on the road, while he opened to us the Scriptures?" ... *Then he opened* [the disciples'] *minds to understand the Scriptures...*

Luke 24:32, 45

the men on the road to Emmaus'
hearts burning within

When is the last time your heart burned within you? When did you last seem to see with new eyes, like a light was suddenly flicked on in your soul? When is the last time you had the feeling that you were standing on a precipice – where a fresh understanding of Jesus or Scripture or humans lay before you as entirely unexplored terrain?

Jesus' opening the minds of these two men to the Scriptures caused their hearts to *burn*: a fiery image of both *light* and *heat*. Yes, just as it first brought light and heat to our planet, the Voice of God is ever-speaking Light and Heat into this world.

Over time, the regular opening of ourselves to the Word of God in the Scriptures *will* produce some kind of Light and Heat in our hearts. If you find yourself regularly opening the Scriptures only to experience neither heat nor light, do not fear! Consider a slight change of posture: Rather than relying on your best efforts to pry open the Scriptures, quietly ask Jesus to use the Scriptures to pry *you* open.

Let us, for a moment, delineate the Light and the Heat. Perhaps we may think of the Light of Scripture as primarily *intellectual* enlightenment, as knowledge or insight, as a changed way of *thinking*, as when our *minds* are changed about ourselves, God, or others.

And then let us think of the Heat of Scripture as predominantly a *heart-felt* conviction, as emotional honesty, as willful response, as when our *hearts* are changed about ourselves, God, or others.

Aren't most of us drawn to one more than to the other?

When a person prefers Light and shuns Heat, she engages Scripture *intellectually*, allowing her mind to be penetrated by new ideas. But, alas! There it stays. The mind enlarges while

164

the heart withers. Her heart remains dull and sterile; it does not embrace the sweeping, transformative changes to which God beckons her.

Her approach to Scripture begs the question: When is the last time something you learned in the Scriptures actually *warmed your heart*? When is the last time your heart (and eyes) brimmed with compassion, with Love, with Hope?

When a person prefers Heat and shuns Light, she engages Scripture *emotionally* and with all her *willpower*, finding a cozy gem of feel-good morality inside every Scriptural stone. Intellectual laziness leads to an obsession with out-of-context quotations that smack of triteness. Her philosophies about God, herself, and others remain irrelevantly black-and-white; she suffers from spiritual absent-mindedness; she has neither vim nor vigor necessary to withstand more than a slight tropical breeze.

Her approach to Scripture begs the question: When is the last time something you learned in the Scriptures actually *blew your mind*? When is the last time your brain nearly hurt from an upheaval of its basic ways of thinking about God, about life, about humanity?

Equal parts of Heat and Light are found perhaps nowhere more succinctly than in open-minded, open-hearted prayer. Some might call this contemplative prayer; it is the type of prayer that lets the Heat and Light into one's innermost places. It is here that we find the salvific refinement of our whole selves -- our minds *and* our hearts repenting and believing in concert. It is here that we allow the Light to shine into every corner of our lives, that we dare to draw ever-nearer to the Heat that thaws us from the inside out. It is here that we find our *whole selves*, our *whole lives* changing before our very eyes.

Prayer: <u>Turn up the Heat! Turn on the Light! I need both.</u> Give me the courage to welcome both the Heat and the Light to my innermost places.

Jesus himself stood among them and said to them, "Peace be with you!"
But they were startled and frightened and thought they saw a spirit.
And he said to them, "Why are you troubled, and why do doubts arise in your hearts?
See my hands and feet, that it is I myself."

Luke 24:36-39

Jesus' *peace*

Luke gives us four absolutely delectable words for what we usually call worry, fear, doubts, or anxiety: *startled, frightened, troubled,* and *doubtful.* What is it that you worry about most? Imagine yourself in the center of that inner turmoil for a moment. And then...

Into the middle of all of our doubts, our troubles, the things that concern and smother and worry us, Jesus speaks, simply: Peace be to you! See my hands and my feet, that it is I myself.

Peace be to you: Let there be wholeness in your life.

169

peace: *(Greek) eiréné*, literally to tie together into a whole; when all essential parts are joined together; God's gift of wholeness; peace of mind; an invocation of peace; a common Jewish farewell; in the Hebraistic sense: the health or welfare of an individual

We might get a better sense of Jesus' meaning of "Peace!" if we use instead our word "*Wholeness!*" Yes, it is a bit clunky as a greeting, isn't it? But it is much more fitting in our context because it brings to our minds more of the deep sense of wellness in one's whole person to which Jesus inferred. It is an appeal to end of all of the frittering habits that wreck our daily peace: our obsessive playing and re-playing of a million worst-case scenarios, our compulsive comparing and re-comparing ourselves with others, and our never-ending task lists of things to do to better ourselves and keep up appearances. "Settle," it calls. "Tie together all of your loose ends of discontent, anxiety, and self-deprecation and be at peace within -- for everyone's sake."

See my hands and my feet: The marks remain; the cross was real. I really suffered to death.

It is as if Jesus is identifying with us in our human experience, and inviting us to identify with him in his. "I, too, was startled and frightened; I was troubled and doubting. I know what it was like to be you, to live through what you're living through, to want so desperately to jump out of the train wreck that is your life but to have to hold on through it. I know what it is like to be fully human, to be you. So pour your heart out. Grab on tightly to my nail-pierced hands. Lean your pretty, fretting head on my torn-to-shreds side. These scars are merely visible evidence of the deep woundedness in my heart for you. When no one else possibly can, you can trust that I understand. I know. I'll catch you."

...*that it is I myself*: It's ok. It's just me.

Jesus says: "It's me -- the Person you got to know at dinner and along the dusty paths of everyday life. It's me -- the Person you partied with when times were good and abandoned when times got hard. It's OK. I'm here. I'm still just me. When you're feeling anything but peaceful wholeness, I'll be here. When your best intentions are thwarted by doubt, *I'll be here with you*, in the very midst of it. When you're losing your mind in the chaos, I'll be there – with you – more *present* than ever."

Prayer: <u>Peace to me! See His hands and His feet, that it is Him Himself.</u> The next time I'm: startled, frightened, troubled, or doubtful. Help me to hear anew your invocation to wholeness.

And while they still disbelieved for joy and were marveling...

Luke 24:41

the disciples' *disbelief for joy*

I'll admit it: I'm a disbeliever. But it is not all too often that I disbelieve for joy. No. Quite naturally and unrestrainedly, I disbelieve for entitlement, anger, ungratefulness, or injustice in my heart.

Perhaps disbelief for *those* reasons sounds something like this:

I can't believe I didn't get the promotion I deserved, the money we were owed, or the recognition I earned.

I can't believe my friends are so selfish, my family is so dysfunctional, or my kids are so much trouble.

175

I can't believe what a mess this world is, how narrow-minded people are, or how open-minded people are.

It has always fascinated me that God chooses not to be the kind of God who instantly and surgically extracts disbelief, even from a willing heart, and even when it concerns disbelief about Himself. I suppose that it is because it is not His ultimate aim to turn humans into robots, into persons who are no longer persons but automatons. (After all, if we are to remain believing organisms, we must also be capable of disbelief about *something*, somewhere. And if we are honest with ourselves, we must also admit that we are always still wrestling with disbelief about *something*, somewhere.) Rather, God chooses to be the kind of God who does the slow, gradual, persevering work of human transformation – through his death turned to Life, and through our death turned to Life. He changes us – still disbelievers – into the kind of people who disbelieve for an entirely different reason: for *joy*.

Perhaps disbelief for *joy* sounds something like this:

I can't believe how Good he is to me, to us, to humans.

I can't believe how he uses even small and ugly things to bring about enormous beauty.

I can't believe how his vast Love keeps the world, every second, from falling apart.

Disbelieved for joy fairly perfectly describes the kind of getting-me-out-of-a-rut breakthroughs I have come to expect in my life with God. The sources of my disbelief are varied; the reason for my disbelief seems always to be some version of joy. At times I can't believe my thinking about something was so severely incongruent with reality. Other times I look back at my completely self-centered heart in utter disbelief. At still other times I can't believe the person, thing, or circumstance which God chose to use to teach and humble me: it seemed so unlikely, or so inconsequential, or so dire, or so dark.

Perhaps most of all, I find myself disbelieving for joy how immense is his Grace. There are moments in this life – some that are quite transcendent, others that are quite mundane – in which I get just a partial view of all of the ways that God has saved, is saving, and will potentially save me. From minor missteps to major decisions that turned out even better than I ever could have imagined, from small discomforts to large tragedies, from happy and successful seasons to sad times full of failure, God is orchestrating my life. And His primary reservoir is one of an undergirding, overarching Grace.

Prayer: Oh Lord, I will always be disbelieving. <u>Turn my disbelieving from ungrateful self-pitying to joyful marveling.</u>

See my hands and my feet, that it is I myself.
Touch me, and see. For a spirit does not have
flesh and bones as you see that I have."
And when he had said this,
he showed them his hands and his feet.
...he said, "Have you anything here to eat?"
They gave him a piece of broiled fish, and he
took it and ate before them.

Luke 24:39-43

Jesus' *touchable,*
feedable humanness
'Touch me,' and, 'Let's eat!'

A nd with that, in one fell swooping sentence, the back-to-life Jesus banished any of our snobbish, over-spiritualized notions we might have had that life after death will be all spiritual and no material.

Most of us, at least most of us who are a bit religious, have a touch of Gnosticism lurking in our hearts. Gnosticism is that pesky leaning of the human heart toward assuming that the most important things in the world are 'spiritual things' (i.e. praying, reading the Bible, going to church, singing in church, giving money to church) and that anything that one might not expect to find a monk doing (i.e. eating delicious food, brewing beer, drinking wine, making love, tapping his foot to blues at a bar, hugging his transgendered friend) ought to be shirked. (Not that most of us really ever intend to shirk any of those things. We just live with the lingering guilt that that is precisely what we ought to do.)

It is, indeed, much tidier to divide our lives into two categories: spiritual and material. But such a practice is dishonest. And it tragically bifurcates our thinking – we are unwittingly led to a prideful idealism that then insists, tyrannically, on labeling things as either 'good' or 'bad.'

Furthermore, we love to label people. If they agree with, think like, raise their kids like, and laugh at the same jokes as us, we smack the good label on them. If they treat us or ours rudely, make choices of which we don't approve, we smack the bad label on them.

Jesus didn't differentiate. He let all things be both spiritual and physical, both potentially good and bad. This back-to-life Jesus was decidedly *not* a Gnostic. He was a hugger. And He was one of those people who you actually hope will drop in at any time, the kind of person who finds himself at home at every party. He was the guy who always brings drinks to share, says a genuine "hello" to each person in the house, and then heads straight for your fridge. "Touch me!" And, "Have you anything here to eat?"

Come to think of it, this back-to-life-again Jesus sounds an awful lot like one of my friends, one of the most easily likeable guys in the world and a person I can barely party without: "C'm'ere!" he pulls me in for a whole-hearted hug. A sincere smile wrinkles the corners of his eyes. "It smells amazing in here! What's for dinner?" Then he launches into another one of his stories. Stories in which he is never the hero, but always the dumb goofball. Stories that make everyone - even the most stoic among us – fall to the floor, laughing.

I threw a party recently for some friends and friends of friends. I am almost positive that my former self (the Gnostic, overly-religious one) would have hated it: it had lots of very different people, just the right amount of soiree, and quite a bit of happy cursing. Incidentally, I think the back-to-life Jesus may have loved it: it had lots of very different people, just the right amount of delectable food and drink, welcome hugs and goodbye kisses, and no hate.

I don't pretend to know all that we'll be doing in our lives after our lives on earth, but it sounds like we'll definitely still be touching/hugging

183

and eating! Splendid! Two of the most spiritual things in my life.

Prayer: Cheers! I can't wait to party in person with You. In the meantime, <u>help me to be a "C'm'ere!" and "Let's eat!" kind of person to the people around me.</u>

Then he led them out as far as Bethany, and lifting up his hands he blessed them. While he blessed them, he parted from them and was carried up into heaven.

Luke 24:50-51

Jesus'
blessing

Few contemporary Protestants do much of this so-called 'blessing,' at least in the western world. Nor do we generally have a very high opinion of it. We have trained ourselves to be far too smart for pious sacramentals, far too intellectually-leaning to believe in such mishmash as a blessing making a difference in a person's life, far too skeptical to accept such childlike notions.

Catholics, Eastern Christians, some western charismatics, and, well, Jesus, generally have a much more well-developed understanding and, consequently, a much higher appreciation for blessing others. We have much to learn from them.

My husband's grandmother, a devout Roman Catholic, recently passed. Among her belongings, in a tiny manila envelope were two tokens: a Madonna and a crucifix. The outside of the envelope read, "This Medal was blessed by Our Holy Father Pope John Paul II on October 10, 1993." My mother-in-law mailed them to – of all people – her son and me. My husband and I, decent Protestants but terrible Catholics, had a very invigorating conversation about it. "What are we supposed to do with these?" it began. "I have no idea," it ended. The Medals happened to arrive at our house while I was in the middle of reading a book about Eastern Christian practice and tradition. One day I read:

"What we must bear in mind is that the purpose and meaning of an icon is to help us reach Christ... What is the use of icons? Icons can be a useful aid for some people in the ascent toward God...the senses can be of assistance in our efforts. Just as putrid images that assault our senses can stir up putrid passions, so icons can have the exact opposite effects. When we contemplate icons, good and wholesome holy meanings are created within us. A human being, you see, is not just soul and spirit but also mind, imagination, feelings, senses. It is the whole person that strives to reach God. We find these aids in the Old as well as in the New Testament and they are always available to us as long as we have not reached our destination in unison with God." [1]

I kept the Medals, and gladly.

* * * * * *

In that magical twilight before slumber consumes our children's bedroom, I often lay beside my kids, intending to pray for them. But some nights I just can't; I get choked up just thinking about how desperately I love them, how embarrassingly fond of them I am, and how impossibly ridiculous it is to attempt to put into any sort of words all that I hope, dream, and pray for them. In those moments, it seems all I can do is find a temple/cheek/hair in the dark, put my hand on them, and bless them.

It is not a casual, sluggish, "Oh, well, I guess, for lack of anything better to say: God bless you!" No. It is a whole-hearted, viscerally intentional, "God bless this human." I suppose what I mean, and what I might venture to pray if my eyelids were not so droopy is, "God, confer what is most Beneficial -- in the fullest meaning of the word -- on this small person's life. Make and re-make her, day by day, into more and more of the woman you intend her to

189

be. Build his character, expand his inner life, and strengthen his primary relationships. Help me, likewise, to be an agent of similar Benefit in her everyday life. Make and re-make me into the best good parent I can be for her. I'm *with him* often, even though it's a lot of just doing homework and the dishes. You chose us to live, eat, play, grow together – him for me, me for him – let that be one of the truest blessings of his life. Amen."

Prayer: <u>Bless him. Bless her. Bless our home. Bless our life.</u> Help me to know, to see, to do, to be a blessing to the people around me at every opportunity.

[1] Markides, Kyriacos C. *The Mountain of Silence*. pg 74, 76-77.

And they worshiped him and returned to Jerusalem with great joy...

Luke 24:52

the disciples'
returning with great joy

The finale: *great joy.*
Finally: the only truly appropriate response to a dead God becoming undead.

Every year, each of us, in our own way, mourn the dead Jesus of Lent.

And then, every year, each of us, in our own way, attend to the empty tomb, to the alive Jesus of UnLent.

Every year I find myself responding to it all a bit differently. It all depends on my attention span, my spiritual stamina and immaturities, the circumstances of my life at the moment, my overarching mood, my caffeine intake.

In his book *Surprised by Hope*, N.T. Wright makes the case that we celebrate the alive Jesus for far too short a time, with far less gusto than is warranted. We bury ourselves in the self-denying darkness of death for 40 days and then, upon finding the Empty Tomb, we smell a lily, spend part of one afternoon eating scalloped potatoes, and then call it *done*?!

Yes, a full forty days linger between the Sunday of Resurrection and the day of Jesus' Ascension. What if we, for Wright's, for Jesus', for all our sakes, found ways to celebrate the undoing of Lent -- commemorating all of the visible and invisible ways in which Jesus undid -- and is still undoing -- Death? In our home, I've named it UnLent.[1]

And then, of course, comes the return to our regular lives: to the 285 days or so between the Ascension and next Lent. We must return. There is nowhere else to go.

And so, as I watch Jesus' followers flit back to Jerusalem with great joy, a question loiters in my mind:

How can we possibly live as people burgeoning with great joy even in the midst of the ongoing

194

deaths and hells of this earth?

I cannot, amidst the boredom and unforeseen trials of those 285 days, maintain the happy emotion with which I usually associate *joy*. But I can practice the spiritual discipline of gratefulness that leads to the deep joy of soul: the joy that simmers long and perseveres, the joy that remains stalwartly, even when it insists on a melancholic filter, even when its focus is a bit frazzled.

Ronald Rolheiser argues that gratitude is a primary and necessary source of such *joy*. He writes, "Live with gratitude and thank your Creator by enjoying your life. ...our gratitude is meant to carry... enjoyment of the gift that is given to us. The highest compliment we can give a gift giver is to enjoy the gift thoroughly. We owe it to our Creator to appreciate things, to be as happy as we can be."[2]

Don't we all just want to grow up to be people who return gratefully to our *regular lives* with joy? I do. I want to be a person who rests in the grateful enjoyment of today. I want to be a person who lives more and more out of the joy of what I already *have* -- even in the midst of the Monday thru Friday work of slogging away to make the world around me a more orderly, more beautiful, and less-painful place.

I have found that the older I get, the more disappointed I am with getaways and vacations. It is not that they are so awful or that I dread them; it is just that I have a growing fondness for my Monday thru Friday life.

Prayer: God, cease my urgent longing and anxious anticipation for the emotional froth and intellectual ecstasy of weekends, holidays, and sacred seasons. Rather, <u>fill my everyday days with more sweetness, more joy, more satisfaction, and more brimming-over contentment.</u>

[1] In Appendix III, you will find some ideas for celebrating UnLent at your house. I've brainstormed 40 simple ways to commemorate the undoing of Death itself, particularly during the 40 sacred days between Resurrection and Ascension.

[2] Rolheiser, Ronald. *Sacred Fire: A Vision for Deeper Christian and Human Maturity.*

Appendix I:
Suggested Practices for Advent

1. *Listen.*

• Listen to Luke 1:5-2:40. Read it aloud to yourself or play an audio Bible. Then sit in silence for 2 minutes. Afterward, write down any themes you observed or thoughts you had while listening, related or not.

• Listen to Tchaikovsky's Nutcracker Suite, Handel's Messiah, or another Christmas musical piece that is meaningful to you. Let your mind, heart, and soul be wrapped up with the rapturous beauty of the music.

2. *Memorize.* Memorize one of the following. Write it out in your journal along with why you chose it.

• Luke 1:38 "I am the Lord's servant. May it be to me as you have said."

• Luke 2:29-32 "Lord, now you are letting your servant depart in peace, according to your word; for my eyes have seen your salvation that you have prepared in the presence of all peoples, a light for revelation to the Gentiles, and for glory to your people Israel."

• Luke 2:34-35 "Behold, this child is appointed for the fall and rising of many in Israel, and for a sign that is opposed (and a sword will pierce through your own soul also), so that thoughts from many hearts may be revealed."

3. *Sing.* Read the Magnificat (my soul magnifies) of Mary (Luke 1:46-55) and the song of Zachariah (Luke 1:68-79) side by side. Read them several times over, each time with a different lens. This may be done in several different sittings, one per day, as time allows. The following are a few suggested lenses through which to consider them.

• Read them – or sing them! – as lyrics that were sung. (If you can carry a tune, and feel so inclined, turn on an instrumental piece with whose melody you are already familiar and sing the words of each to the tune being played.)

• Read them as prayed prayers.

• Read them as theological discourses.
• Read them and analyze them for their dom-

inant themes, keywords, and overall tone.

• Read them as the instinctual, bursting-with-love parental response (Mary, newly pregnant; Zechariah, a newly unmuted new dad with babe-in-arms).

4. *Pay attention to fear.* Read or listen to Luke 1:5-2:40. Pay attention to the role of fear in the story of Jesus' birth. "Fear not!" It is the angels' repeated refrain. It shows up in a line in Zachariah's poem: "...that we might serve him without fear..." How does the Advent of God hold the potential to allay all of your fears?

5. *Contemplate unexpectedness.* Make a list of all of the ways that Jesus' first coming was un-expected. Dare to put yourself in the place of the Father for a moment.

• How might you have proposed to solve the problem of "war on earth, ill-will among men?" How, when, and in what form would you have sent your God-Human Prince to solve the problem? To whom would you have first announced his arrival? Why?

• In what ways do you find the ways of God as seen in Advent to be not at all like what you'd expect?

• Bonus points if you: Imagine how Jesus' second coming might be just as unexpected as his first.

6. *Be quiet.* Find a quiet and private place that is beautiful to you (an open church sanctuary, a vista from your parked car, a corner of your study or bedroom) in which to sit for quiet reflection and prayer. Put aside any potential distractions; bring your journal. Sit, kneel, or stand for 20 minutes in silence. Feel free to jot down any words or brief thoughts in your journal, but try not to let the silence be consumed with journaling. If desired, return later to the phrases you scribbled down to write more about how you heard, saw, and experienced God in the silence.

7. *Be alone.* Bundle up (if you're in the Northern Hemisphere!) and go for a prayer walk outside. Before you head out the door, invite God to interrupt, weigh in on, and direct your thoughts. Then just let your mind prayerfully wander. Don't try to keep your attention on God. Just loosen up and consider all of your thoughts to be prayer. Listen to the snow crunch. Feel the cold bite at your exposed parts. Think about all of the ways (physical, metabolic, microscopic, intellectual, spiritual) that God's Presence

keeps you warm in the midst of such cold.

8. *Imagine.* Choose a person from the birth story of Jesus and read the narrative again, imagining yourself in their shoes. (Matthew 1:18-2:23 or Luke 1:5-2:40 are good candidates.) What would you have been thinking? How would you have felt? What would have been your kneejerk response to each event as it unfolded? What would you have done or not done?

9. *Celebrate friendship.* Choose 12 friends and write each one a handwritten Christmas card. Tell them what you actually think about and feel toward them. It need not be long; it need be only personal and sincere. Give them the gift of not expecting them to write back.

10. *Reflect.* Near the close of the day, sit next to your Christmas tree. Let the lights on the tree be the only lights on around you. Consider the following two questions:

  • When today did I sense and welcome the Advent of God (God dwelling with me)?
  • At what moments during my day did I, like Herod, resist the Advent of God?

11. *Observe the heart of a child.* Spend a couple of hours with a child, preferably 18 months to

8 years old. (Bonus points if you: Borrow some-one else's child, thereby giving a dear young parent a perhaps much-needed and definitely much-appreciated break!) Watch a Christmas movie together, drink hot cocoa with a peppermint in it, take turns guessing what is in each wrapped gift beneath the tree, go on a car ride to see Christmas lights, sing carols along the way, etc. Pay attention. Ask questions. Listen carefully. Prayerfully discern what they're thinking and how they're feeling. Experience some wonder together. Write down your observations, impressions, thoughts, and epiphanies at the end of the day.

12. *Practice generosity.* As the wise men did at Jesus' birth, practice costly generosity. To what person in your life this Christmas do you least feel like giving a gift? Take time to think of something that they would like. Purchase it for them. Wrap it beautifully. Give it anonymously, if possible.

Appendix II:
Suggested Practices for Lent

Suggested practices for Lent are easy to find; Lent is the time of year when perhaps the largest percentage of Christ-followers practice some form of asceticism en mass. Foregoing chocolate, caffeine or entertainment can be an excellent reflection of the death-to-self that characterizes the Jesus of Lent.

The following is a little invention of mine to practice the six weeks of Lent. It is a bit unconventional, perhaps especially helpful for shedding new light (or new darkness?!) on Lenten practices that may have begun to feel routine.

Lent, culminating in Jesus' crucifixion, is marked by *invisibility* & *anonymity*, *ugliness*, *vulnerability* & *nakedness*, *pain*, *dusk*, and *darkness*. For our practice, each of the six Lenten weeks will employ one of the above as its theme. The practice is simple: wear or keep with you something that reflects the week's theme, and let that thing serve as a reminder of the theme throughout the day. Use the suggested contemplations and prayers to keep the theme always in the back of your mind.

Week 1

Begin on Ash Wednesday. Each new week will begin on the following Wednesday.

Theme: *Jesus' invisibility, anonymity, and forgottenness*

Thesis: Jesus' betrayal and abandonment by dear friends compassionately touches our loneliness and beckons us to see and remember every human being.

Wear or keep with you each day: something clear or transparent (i.e. earrings, eyeglass frames, watch band, water bottle, travel mug)

Let your clothing or accessory remind you to contemplate throughout the week:

• In what ways do you sometimes feel anonymous, invisible, or betrayed?

• What things in your everyday life often go unnoticed, and therefore unappreciated? What things from the natural world do you sometimes take for granted that reflect God's value of anonymity and forgottenness? (i.e. white blood cells, pharmaceuticals, unlovely people, uninteresting people)

Week 2

Theme: *Jesus' ugliness, in life and in death*

Thesis: Sometimes ugly things are necessary to make other things functional and beautiful.

Wear or keep with you each day: something you consider to be ugly

Contemplate throughout the week:

• What ugly things serve to make life more orderly, more functional, and more beautiful? (i.e. feet, mouth guards or retainers, messy or ugly rooms in my home, fights: ugly communication that clears the air and brings darkness into the light)

Week 3

Theme: *Jesus' vulnerability and nakedness*

Thesis: Jesus, the Perfect Human, modeled costly vulnerability toward God and others.

Don't wear or keep with you each day: something you would say you feel 'naked' without (i.e. phone, waterbottle, cup of coffee, handbag, watch, jewelry, baseball cap, underclothes)

Whenever you realize you don't have with you the item you always have with you, use the reminder to contemplate:

• What does relational, spiritual, and emotional nakedness look like in a world that is usually so buttoned up? How can vulnerability be the Way of Jesus when it feels so frighteningly risky in our "safety first" world?

• What is beautiful about vulnerability? What is beautiful about nakedness?

• What on earth would it look like to move our lives in the direction of the creation poem that rendered humankind "naked [and vulnerable] and without shame"?

210

Week 4

Theme: *Jesus' pain*

Thesis: The inclusion of pain in Jesus' flawlessly lived life emphatically massacres the "good things happen to good people" prosperity gospel.

Wear or keep with you each day: black and blue together, like a bruise

Whenever someone comments on your black and blue mismatch, contemplate:

• Jesus' perfectly lived life was wrought with pain and ended in brutal pain.

• How does the perfect pain of Jesus offer to change our perspective on our pain?

• In what ways is pain good?

Week 5

Theme: *dusk*

Thesis: The impeccable life of Jesus, "man of sorrows," was a life lived in the twilight of continual descent, growing darker and darker until it reached the point of pitch black.

Wear or keep with you each day: something brown or gray

Did someone say you were looking drab? Congratulations! Be reminded in that moment to contemplate:

- In what areas does life feel like a continual dusk, a humble descent?

- Pray: God help us to celebrate the dusky, not-so-bright parts of life as the Way of Jesus. Keep us from missing out on the goodness of a drab life. Show us the hope to be found in twilight, not only in the sunrise.

Week 6

Theme: *darkness*

Thesis: Is anything darker and more despairing than utter abandonment by God? Jesus experienced such darkness on Golgotha: hell on earth.

Wear or keep with you each day: something black

Contemplate throughout the week:

• Are there areas of life in which you feel stuck in hopeless darkness?

• Will you continue to cry out? Will you remain open to God even when the only answer you get is silence?

• Look for characteristics of the natural world that reflect God's inclusion of and openness toward the darkness. Find the good in the darkness. (i.e. the pitch blackness of night, the blackness of deep water, the blackness of a deep hole in the ground)

Appendix III:
Suggested Practices for UnLent

1. Bring new life to your yard or home by planting a tree or buying a houseplant. Tend it with care.

2. Rekindle your interest in an old hobby you haven't enjoyed in quite some time.

3. Research that topic or learn how to do that thing in which you've always been interested but have never taken the time to learn: i.e. botany, badgers, ballet, bowling, Bali...

4. Bring new life to an old friendship: Write a note to a friend with whom you've lost touch.

5. Start a conversation with a new person at work, school, or store. "I know we've seen each other around a lot; we've just never officially met. My name is.."

6. Go to a bookstore; smell a new book.

7. Give something old a fresh coat of paint.

8. Who have been the three most life-giving people in your life (past or present)? Write each a handwritten note, telling them so.

9. Make a list of six ways you've seen God breathe fresh life into you in the last six months.

10. Make a list of six more ways you've seen God breathe fresh life into you in the last six hours.

11. Make a list of six more ways you've seen God breathe fresh life into you in the last six minutes.

12. Drink a mimosa with breakfast. Be sure to offer Cheers! to a God who became a baby, brutally died, and then showed that forever-life is possible by coming back to life!

13. Plan a getaway with someone who is life-giving for you; something to look forward to in the next 6 months.

14. Carve out time in these 40 days to read a book you've always wanted to read.

15. Buy a gift for a friend or family member 'just because' - something that you know will be life-giving for them.

16. Read a book you would not ordinarily consider reading. Perhaps new life will come from an unexpected source!

17. Visit a workplace not your own. Ask God to use the visit to give you fresh ideas and fresh vision for work and rest, community and love.

18. Give financially to an organization that offers new life to the people it serves.

19. Listen for a few hours to a different genre of music than you usually do.

20. Take a personality test with a coach, sign up for a class, or register for therapy: Let the Spirit of God take you to new and deeper levels of self-awareness.

21. Try a new food – the riskier, the better! Your pallate matures every five years; maybe you'll like something now that you didn't like in the past.

22. Read a biography of someone who inspires you.

23. Read a chapter book aloud with your kids, your relatives, or your friends: something that will really get your imaginations going!

24. Set aside some quiet time to imagine your life 5 years from now. Jot down some of your hopes, dreams, goals. Do the same for 10 years from now and 25 years from now.

25. Buy a new-to-you grain, vegetable, or sauce at the grocery store that you have no idea how to cook. Research how to cook it and give it a try!

26. Take a new route on your next neighborhood walk, run for exercise, or commute to work.

27. Think of a person who you don't like very much. Commit to pray a one-sentence prayer for new life for them each day of these 40 days.

28. Keep fresh flowers on a vase on your dining table for these 40 days. Whenever they start looking wilty, buy new!

29. Eat one piece of your favorite chocolate every single day for these 40 days.

30. Write a poem, paint on canvas, or build something with your hands that expresses artistically what new life means to you.

31. Adopt a new pet.

32. Prayerfully contemplate: How might I bring life to someone around me whose life is a kind of hell on earth right now?

33. Brainstorm one small change to your regular weekly schedule that would make each week more life-giving to you and to your family, immediate or extended. (Consider taking something out, putting something in, or altering something slightly.)

34. Play with a spiritual discipline you haven't tried until now. Look for suggestions in Adele Ahlberg Calhoun's *Spiritual Disciplines Handbook: Practices that Transform Us*.

35. Pray every day of the 40 days: God, show me how Jesus' coming back to life makes a difference in my life today.

36. Read *Surprised by Hope* by N.T. Wright.

37. Memorize Ephesians 2:1-10.

38. Meditate on the following Scriptures about life, keeping in mind that for their original audience, eternal life meant living the fullest life today, not going to heaven when you die: Deuteronomy 30:19-20; Psalm 16; Psalm 30:3; John 3:14-17 (Numbers 21:4-9).

39. Sign up to mentor a child through a local community organization.

40. Bring new life into your home by fostering or adopting a child!

Epilogue

With *Passions Trilogy*, I join the multitudinous devotional writers of our modern age, an age in which spiritual devotionals have fairly blossomed like wildflowers, spreading themselves indiscriminately across the hillsides of Christ-following thought and practice. Isn't it a beautiful and variegated field?!

At times, I feel incredibly presumptuous to offer to you my little collection of devotionals – after all, isn't a devotional just a bunch of meandering thoughts and, at best, a few spiritual insights on a Scriptural text? But most of the time, I feel supremely humbled and honored to offer it to you, even a little devotional collection – after all, don't we desperately need to listen to each other in order to grow and mature and change? If, perhaps, one little thought of mine would plant itself in your very heart and if, perhaps, that thought would grow by the invisible, uncontainable Spirit of God into more Peace on earth, Goodwill toward men, then I will count all my work as having been worthwhile.

In the meantime, these passions have embedded themselves into my very heart, germinating and growing and spreading out like so much wiry angel vine. Perhaps, in the extravagantly generous economy of the kingdom of God, that alone is enough.

In the meantime, I feel proud to be part of a society that continues to open its ears to allow more and more voices to join in the conversation, to open its arms to welcome whatever gifts one brings to the table, and to open its heart to the brokenhearted, the oppressed, the silenced in love. What else did Jesus come to do than that? Why else do we read devotionals if not to let the Spirit of God open us up more in all of those ways? We have still a very far way to go – until every creature is enfolded in his steadfast Love – but, at least on most days, I am just brazen enough to believe that God remains stalwartly salvific in his work in this world, and that therefore he has us headed in many of the right directions. I am an artist; I simply must continue to brazenly believe or, sadly, all of my work will fail and, unrecuperatively, all of my God will fail with it.

In the meantime, I think that the best devotionals do three things. First, they unleash one's imagination until one's feet are firmly planted in the shoes of another – be he good or bad, saintly or cranky, or both at once. Second, they corner one's soul into the awe-ful awfulness of self-reflection. These two things together give birth to the third thing: Love. Don't we who read devotionals read them because we have a deep longing in our souls to love God more, and to feel the nearness of that Love? Isn't that Love all that we truly need? Isn't it what we want most singularly?

With that, I proudly join this ever-expanding cloud of devotional writers, mere witnesses of the God who is Love. And I say: Let us give birth to Love: for God and for others! Let Love be our rallying cry through the three predominant liturgical seasons. Let Love be our singular measurement of a 'successful completion' of the devotionals laid out here. Let Love be enough for us, and let our thirst for it and for its Source never be quenched. Let each of us, in the end, continue on our own way, bolstered by Love: by his indiscriminate, without-conditions, never-tiring, tenacious Love for us and by our ever-burgeoning Love for Him, for Goodness' sake.

Author's Note

A few Christmases ago, a dear friend gifted me a beautiful advent devotional – a series of artful cards with a paragraph or two from the Advent narrative to read each day. The cards hung on a string to make a garland. I loved it. It was so inspiring, so pleasurable to look at, and I relished them during the few short weeks between that Thanksgiving and Christmas.

The next summer, seven months pregnant with our third child, I decided to purge a bunch of storage boxes in the basement. I stumbled upon the devotional cards and lifted them gingerly out of a Christmas box. My husband caught me gazing at them in childlike wonder, with tingly-sacred fingertips.

"You should write your own," he said, simply, plainly.

I just looked at him, silenced by his audacity. He knew how I'd loved them. He saw the ways that they had awakened the artist in me. He must've been listening when I'd whined to him a thousand times, "I think I'm supposed to be writing, like it's a calling God has imprinted on me. But, I just... I mean... how can I ever find the time? I mean I hardly sleep and there're these little kids of ours who live with us day in and day out..."

Did he actually now believe that I could do it? I realized in a moment that I didn't believe I could do it.

"When could you have it done?" he persisted, ignoring my excuses for the thousand-and-first time. It was almost a dare. I just looked at him. "How about October 31," he said. It wasn't a question.

"Are you telling me what to do?" I teased, still mesmerized by the cards. "Don't tell me what to do."

"Well you're saying you need to write and I know how much you loved those advent devotionals, so write your own."

How does he see all of this so plainly? I marveled.

It was as if he held in his hands the self-confidence and artistic audacity that I needed, but that I didn't posses myself. And now he was

228

holding them out to me, humbly, generously, emboweringly.

"Maybe I will," I said. And in that moment I knew that I would.

So there it was, sitting on the table before me. Not yet begun. My first real writing project.

And so, three years later, here it is, sitting on the table before you. Done. My first real writing project.

It has multiplied significantly in those three years.

I wrote the first twelve devotionals, *Passions of Christ's Birth*, while I was on maternity leave with that third baby. Those months were full of an ease and a joy uncharacteristic for maternity leave, at least in my limited experience. And then, as the year of liturgical seasons came and went in my heart over the next few years, it seemed fitting for my *Passions of Christ's Birth* devotional to gain two siblings: first a Lenten (*Passions of Christ's Death*) and then an Un-Lenten (*Passions of Christ's Resurrection*) partner.

The two siblings were written early in the morning before the kids woke up, sometimes lying in bed next to a sleeping toddler, sometimes in a coffeeshop while someone else watched the kids for a bit, often on a hard-fought-for mini writing retreat. Most of it was written on my heart, imprinting itself in my mind thought by thought during the hours of just living – doing laundry, changing diapers, eating breakfast, making money, spending money. Then, the thoughts got scribbled down whenever I could make the time.

*   *   *   *   *   *

I share this story because I want to encourage you, dear reader, to continue to live your daily, ordinary life with whole-heartedness and meaning. The origins of the simple book that is before you, my first published work, were far more mundane and haphazard than they were wistful or romantic. To you who are artists, like me, I want you to know that often the best art comes less from what feel like optimal conditions for art and more from what is just real life. To all of you: please keep doing your work, whatever work you are called to do today. Keep learning the Way of Jesus and keep finding your vocation in the midst of that. We need you in this world; we need your best contributions to it.

Acknowledgments

I am sublimely grateful to God for gracing my life with the following humans. Without each of you this book would not exist.

Becky, our effusively loving nanny. Thank you for taking such special care of my kids while I disappeared for a bit to write.

Pam, my humble partner in the constant battle for order against chaos. I simply do not think or create well when my home is filthy. Thank you for blessing me with shiny floors and clean toilets so that I am freer to write.

Nana, my mom, who takes care that everyone is amply fed and watered, whose hospitality is an immense gift, and at whose house my kids feel sublimely at home. Thank you for modeling to me others-centeredness, generosity, and hard work -- they have proven to be invaluable gifts for life, and especially for the work of writing.

Dad: Sometimes when I write I hear your voice in my voice. It's scary and funny and wonderful. Thank you for praying for me always. Thank you for raising me to know God, to love truth, and to live by my principles.

Holly, my only sister, my obligatory therapist, my 52-days-per-year roommate, and (surprise!) one of my very dearest friends. Your willingness to talk endlessly, to listen carefully, and to wrestle bravely alongside me with Life and God and Love keeps my heart and soul alive. Your unwavering belief in me has given me the courage and audacity to turn this vocational corner into the world of writing. There is no one in this world like you, and I'm so glad you're mine.

Doc: Your encouraging words have kept me writing at times when I have desperately wanted to quit. Thank you for cheering for me.

Melissa, Stephanie, and Amanda Fay: With you I have the great gift of being just exactly myself. It is one of the most loving, most freeing experiences of my life. Among friends, what more can one ask or hope? Thanks for reading everything I write, for being genuinely excited to watch me become a writer, and for letting me work out my salvation with and before you. xoxoxo

Tyler: God used your humility and feminism to rescue and heal me from a very dark season. Our conversations regularly expand my brain and my world; our friendship regularly expands my heart. I'm so glad we accidentally met, accidentally worked together, and accidentally became friends.

Diane, Donna, and Carolyn, my trinity of spiritual mentorship and direction. Just knowing that real people like you exist in this world bolsters my hope and trust in God. Thank you for allowing God to do the good, slow, transformative work in you that has caused you to become the women you are today. Thank you for praying for me and for encouraging me to write.

Pam, Rosemary, Laura, and Becca: Thank you so much for reading my manuscript and giving me warm and helpful feedback! Your suggestions were brilliant. Your responses were unbelievably uplifting.

Evelyn, Kathleen, Maria, Madeleine, Beverly, Graham, Richard, Timothy, Tom, Jack, and Eugene, the thinker-writers who continually inspire me. We've never met, and some of you are dead, but I feel as though I know you. Thank you for doing the complex and beautiful work of writing down your thoughts so that I could benefit. Thank you for awakening the writer in me and for setting such high standards!

Howard, Stone, and Wells: You keep me grounded, growing, and happy-in-love. I desperately need all of those things if I'm ever going to grow up to be a writer. Parenting humbly and perpetually centers one's life around Love, and loving you is as easy as pie -- but even more delicious.

Jason: Did you know on that long ago rainy day in May what a good idea our marriage was? Every year I become more and more convinced. I absolutely love eating, dating, partying, raising kids, working, celebrating, dreaming, talking, reading, sleeping, traveling, and living with you. You regularly bring out the fun, the contentedness, and the best in me. You keep our home at peace, restful, freeing, patient, and flexible when I regularly threaten to undo all of those things. I need a life and a home like that if I am going to do work like this. What's more: You sometimes graciously make my projects your projects. You champion women in general and me in particular. You consistently cultivate a culture around you in which others are buoyed up to do and to become all God made them to be. And so: What do you know!? A girl like me is actually becoming a writer. "Thanks," seems like such a lame word for all of that. But: thanks! I absolutely could not, would not have done any of this without you. I love you so.